P9-DZY-996

OSKAR REINHART COLLECTION «AM RÖMERHOLZ» WINTERTHUR

CHRISTINA AND MATTHIAS FREHNER

SWISS MUSEUMS

BANQUE PARIBAS (SUISSE) S.A. IN COOPERATION WITH THE
SWISS INSTITUTE FOR ART RESEARCH

Editor
Swiss Institute for Art Research
(Juerg Albrecht)

Translation from the German
Susan Atherley, Marcia Schoenberg

Editing
Swiss Institute for Art Research
(Regina Bühlmann)
Design
Ewald Graber, Berne
Layout
Swiss Institute for Art Research
(Juerg Albrecht)

Photography
Oskar Reinhart Collection
«Am Römerholz», Winterthur
(Bernhard Nicod, Hans Humm)
Swiss Institute for Art Research
(Jean-Pierre Kuhn)
Photolithography
Schwitter AG, Allschwil / Basle
Setting and printing
Condrau SA, Disentis
Binding
Benziger AG, Einsiedeln

Copyright 1993 by
Swiss Institute for Art Research, Zurich
Banque Paribas (Suisse) S.A., Geneva

ISBN 3-908184-19-3
[English, museum brochure]
ISBN 3-908184-20-7
[English, bound edition]
ISBN 3-908184-15-0
[French, museum brochure]
ISBN 3-908184-16-9
[French, bound edition]
ISBN 3-908184-13-4
[German, museum brochure]
ISBN 3-908184-14-2
[German, bound edition]
ISBN 3-908184-17-7
[Italian, museum brochure]
ISBN 3-908184-18-5
[Italian, bound edition]

9.98 2600 U 42460

Foreword

The present publication was made possible by the patronage of Banque Paribas Suisse. With their series *Swiss Museums*, a lasting contribution has been made to the 700th anniversary celebration of the Swiss Confederation. The volume on the Oskar Reinhart Collection «Am Römerholz» is, after the Museum of Art and History in Geneva and the Museum of Fine Arts in Zurich, the third in the series whose aim it is to provide a representative view of the cultural diversity of Swiss museums. This publication in German, French, Italian and English fulfils the wish to present the brilliant achievement of the collector Oskar Reinhart to a wide national and international public.

The Collection «Am Römerholz» is a well composed ensemble of exquisite works, an overall impression of which is quickly attained. The high quality of the works is, on the other hand, inestimable. The volume conveys to the reader the personality of Oskar Reinhart and highlights the most important aspects of his private collection which he bequeathed to the Swiss Confederation. Its aim is to provide access to an understanding of these art treasures. No text, however, can be a substitute for the art work itself. One of the most prominent visitors to the gallery «Am Römerholz», the poet Paul Valéry, wrote in Oskar Reinhart's visitors' book: «The whole world has spoken about this magnificent collection, but it speaks for itself a hundred times stronger than the world has done.» These words are still valid today.

It is my pleasure to thank: the two authors for the informative text, Banque Paribas Suisse for its generous commitment and the Swiss Institute for Art Research for taking responsibility for the editorial coordination and design of this beautiful book.

Alfred Defago
Director of the Federal Department of Culture

Oskar Reinhart, Art Collector

«Non-artists often have a more elevated understanding of art», wrote the twenty-two year old Oskar Reinhart to his father from London on November 21, 1907, on the occasion of Theodor Reinhart's birthday.[1] This letter was a glowing document of self-defense. The young native of Winterthur, an ongoing businessman, was to be given the finishing touch at the London branch of his father's trading firm. But what enthused him beyond measure was art alone.

That which moved him was far more than the fad of those German students about whom he had previously informed his mother: «Both are studying art and architecture, but neither one of them is capable or knows much about his discipline. In Germany, it makes a good impression if a member of the family can paint!»[2] Oskar Reinhart, however, possessed a sound knowledge. His father, Theodor Reinhart, who not only provided financial support to the «art boys»[3] Karl Hofer, Hermann Haller and others, but also wanted to help them cope with life, showed Oskar and his siblings a personal approach to art. By 1907 Oskar Reinhart had already seen the majority of European museums as well as epochal exhibitions: In 1905 the extensive Vincent van Gogh Exhibition at the Stedelijk Museum, Amsterdam, and in 1906 the Berlin centennial «Exhibition of German Art from the era 1775−1875», organized by Hugo von Tschudi, Alfred Lichtwark and Julius Meier-Graefe.

That which Oskar Reinhart loved, he wanted to possess. His birthday letter to his strict father was a plea for understanding: «After all, it is not enough to simply gaze eternally at the object of one's love, one wants to possess a work of art as one does a treasure and a friend, to have one's educator constantly present.»[4] Art was to him of ideal magnitude, its acquisition a conquest: «I am always proud to bring home a new art work. At first, the financial expenditure rather alarms me, then comes the struggle to which I always succumb when the work is *really good*. But for me this concept is very limited, and therefore one cannot accuse me of being thoughtless in my expenditures. And when I think how much one regains through ownership! [...] Even if the prices fall for this or that, a work by Whistler − or however the artists are all called − will always remain valuable to me if it really is indicative of great art. With passing years its worth even increases, because herein my judgement and my taste were put to the test.»[5]

At that time, Oskar Reinhart was already aware that his interest was reserved for the very few and that art collecting meant more than mere

Hermann Hubacher (1885−1976)
Portrait Bust of Oskar Reinhart. 1935
Bronze. Height 29.5 cm
Purchased 1935

The villa «Am Römerholz»,
seen from the grounds

personal pleasure: «Art and beauty remain, more or less, a privilege of the wealthy; they alone can ever call a portion of these treasures their own. One who only buys old paintings forgets his obligation to his own time; one who supports the superior art of his time is a benefactor of the present, and even more so, of coming generations; and he who defends bad art, which is not art at all, is criminal.»[6] Straightforward words of a twenty-two year old, as is the statement: «For me, to own a single piece of graphic art is necessary compensation for the so frequent spiritual barrenness of my daily surroundings.»[7]

His father had, again and again, to grant him «art loans», and in the following year Oskar asked for an educational sojourn in Berlin: «Perhaps you will be able to understand that having to swallow all this pampered English art, coupled with the deadly one-sidedness of my business training, demands compensation in the form of a few months of intellectual refreshment.»[8] The spring of 1909 found Oskar Reinhart in Berlin. Shortly after his arrival he wrote: «I have already sought out all the art salons: Cassirer, Gurlitt, Schulte, etc.»[9] He not only visited museums but also artists' studios, among them the «greenhouse» where Emil Nolde and his female companion lived and worked. In a letter to his parents Oskar Reinhart wrote: «I know very well that Nolde's art has few admirers; it is, for the most part, rather foreign to me. Nevertheless, one discerns that within these four walls, someone is wrestling and struggling, a man attempting to attain great things by honest means.» And further on: «Papa will not hold it against me for having acquired a few graphic exponents. [...] They really please me from a purely artistic standpoint, and I place them alongside the best works of Munch known to me.»[10]

Oskar Reinhart in India, c. 1910

The «intellectual refreshment» in Berlin was of short duration. On April 23, 1909, Oskar Reinhart boarded the «Egypt» in Marseille and set sail for India to visit the branches of his father's firm «Volkart Brothers» which were established there and where he was to spend the next two years. By April 16, 1911, he was at home again in Winterthur. From then on he worked in his father's firm until 1924 when he withdrew from business life in order to devote himself entirely to his collection.

Statements made by Oskar Reinhart verify that he had long possessed extensive knowledge of art. In whichever metropolis he lingered, doors of the most important private collections were opened to him. Initially, invitations were proffered owing to the world-wide influence of the Volkart Brothers; soon he would be appreciated because of his sensational accuracy in judging artistic quality.

He was influenced considerably by Julius Meier-Graefe's three-volume «Entwicklungsgeschichte der Modernen Kunst» (1904) in which French Impressionism was seen in a new light and elevated to a position it deserved but had hitherto not enjoyed in German-speaking countries, and by Hugo von Tschudi who put these impulses into practice during his museum career (in Berlin and Munich). For Oskar Reinhart, «Artistic quality was identical with painterly merit. For this reason», concludes Eduard Hüttinger, «'Peinture' characterizes the core of the Oskar Reinhart Collection».[11]

In a first phase, Oskar Reinhart concentrated on building up his collection of graphic art, exhibiting it in various exhibitions held at the Kunstmuseum in Winterthur. Beyond that, a statement made by Reinhart in 1914 demonstrated that he visualized his future collection as a «musée imaginaire» long before he systematically began to acquire paintings. The document – with a marginal note: «I am keeping this paper to document my tenets as collector anno 1914» – instructed his «surviving brothers» to obtain works by the «following masters» for the Kunstmuseum in Winterthur: «Rembrandt, Hals, Velázquez, Greco, Goya, Constable, Géricault, Delacroix, Courbet, Daumier, Corot, Daubigny, Manet, Degas, Monet, Renoir, van Gogh, Cézanne, Sisley, Toulouse-Lautrec, Leibl, Trübner, Liebermann, Schuch, Alt, Menzel».[12] This list anticipates not only the chronological scope of his later collection, but also one of its important characteristics: the confrontation of nineteenth century French and German painting.

After his father's death in 1919, Oskar Reinhart moved into his own home in Winterthur and intently set about procuring paintings. To this end, the Winterthur painter, Carl Montag, who had been living in Paris since 1903, played the important role of mediator. The Winterthur circle of collectors, Richard Bühler, Arthur and Hedy Hahnloser-Bühler and the brothers Oskar and Georg Reinhart became familiar with the art of Impressionism, of the Nabis and the Fauves. With the closing of the borders during the First World War, Oskar Reinhart often commissioned Montag to make purchases on his behalf. Hence, at the «Vente Degas», Montag bought Cézanne's *Self Portrait*, at the «Sale Mirbeau» van Gogh's *Still Life of Herrings, Tomatoes and Lemons* and at the «Vente Denis Cortuis» Delacroix's *Tasso in the House of the Insane*.

In the period which followed, Oskar Reinhart usually made his purchases himself. Thanks to his profound knowledge, he made many spec-

[1] OSKAR REINHART, letter to Theodor Reinhart, London, 21 November 1907. Archives of the Oskar Reinhart Collection «Am Römerholz» (AORC).

[2] OSKAR REINHART, letter to Lilly Reinhart, London, 19 April 1907, AORC.

[3] See: URSULA and GÜNTER FEIST in the epilogue for: *Karl Hofer und Theodor Reinhart. Maler und Mäzen. Ein Briefwechsel in Auswahl*, publ. by Ursula and Günter Feist, Berlin 1989, pp. 469–470.

[4] OSKAR REINHART, letter to Theodor Reinhart, London, 21 November 1907, AORC.

[5] OSKAR REINHART, letter to Theodor Reinhart, London, 21 November 1907, AORC.

[6] OSKAR REINHART, letter to Theodor Reinhart, London, 21 November 1907, AORC.

[7] OSKAR REINHART, letter to Theodor Reinhart, London, 21 November 1907, AORC.

[8] OSKAR REINHART, letter to Theodor Reinhart, London, 2 June 1908, AORC.

[9] OSKAR REINHART, letter to Lilly and Theodor Reinhart, Berlin, 12 March 1909, AORC.

[10] OSKAR REINHART, letter to Lilly and Theodor Reinhart, Berlin, 18 March 1909, AORC.

[11] EDUARD HÜTTINGER, *Oskar Reinhart. Historische Prämissen seiner Sammlung*, in: Rudolf Koella, Sammlung Oskar Reinhart Am Römerholz, Winterthur, Zürich 1975, p. 23.

[12] OSKAR REINHART, testimony, Winterthur, 30 April 1914, AORC.

tacular acquisitions. He was one of the first on the spot when the prestigious Hansen Collection was dissolved in Copenhagen and informed his brother Georg that he had been successful in purchasing many priceless works by Delacroix, Corot, Daumier, Millet, Courbet, Manet, Degas, Pissarro, Sisley, Renoir and Cézanne. «The pearls of Hansen's collection are now mine», he wrote, and added, somewhat despondently, «It's a pity that I am unable to hang all these paintings on the walls of my home. I am constantly preoccupied with the problem of how to accommodate my collection.»[13] Oskar Reinhart had, at that time, not only secured numerous nineteenth century French, German and Swiss paintings, but also old masters, from Tintoretto and Rubens to Chardin and Goya.

The Main Gallery

The Renaissance Room, former living-room of Oskar Reinhart, with original furnishings

The problem of space was solved with the acquisition of the imposing villa «Am Römerholz» in 1924. It had been built above the town for a Winterthur industrialist by the Genevan architect Maurice Turrettini. During that same year Turrettini was commissioned to build a gallery. The villa and gallery annex, and its setting within a beautiful park, make up a harmonious ensemble, distinguished by French Neoclassicism. A new life began for Oskar Reinhart at «Römerholz», one in which he could devote himself exclusively to his avocation. The «inner struggle between profession and inclination, between duty and natural talent and interests», which was also the «underlying reason for my bachelorhood», finally came to an end, the collector wrote in an unsent letter to Georg.[14]

His personal vision, the basis of his creative achievement as a collector, began to take shape. Starting with the free play of colour and light of the Impressionists as well as a «spiritual, poetic content» (Max Huggler)[15] which Oskar Reinhart found embodied in their paintings, he discovered these same qualities in the works of earlier periods. Objective and subjective criteria must be in accord with one another: The objective view is that of a businessman who does not allow himself to be carried away, who considers at length, reflects and examines; the subjective view, on the other hand, is that of a muse-inspired dreamer who immerses himself in a work of art in order to sense its message.

Without this accord, he did not buy, no matter how famous a painting may have been. The high quality of all the works found in «Römerholz», representing five centuries, fuses them into an integrated whole

[13] OSKAR REINHART, letter to Georg Reinhart, 26 April 1923, AORC.
[14] OSKAR REINHART, letter to Georg Reinhart, 16 January 1920, AORC.
[15] MAX HUGGLER, *Die Privatsammlung Oskar Reinhart*, in: Schweizer Monatshefte, October 1955, p. 359.

Caspar David Friedrich (1774–1840)
Chalk Cliffs on Rügen. 1818
Oil on canvas. 90 × 70 cm
The Oskar Reinhart Foundation,
Winterthur
Purchased 1930

The Oskar Reinhart Foundation, Winterthur, in the former secondary school, built 1838–1842 by Leonhard Zeugheer

and withstands, with ease, objective criteria. The manner of presentation, decided upon by Oskar Reinhart, has remained basically the same until this day and does not follow the dictates of art history. Rather the works of art have been brought into relationship with each other as a result of personal considerations. Thus, the collector brought about unusual encounters between Rubens and Courbet, Claude Lorrain and Constable, Frans Hals and Goya.

These works were incorporated into the collection mainly during the 1920s and 1930s. Reinhart purchased through art dealers with whom he was on friendly terms, foremost with Fritz Nathan. In later years he acquired a picture only if it had been on his list for some time and became available suddenly. This was the case with Manet's great painting *Au Café* which had been in the Gerstenberg Collection of Berlin and was known to Reinhart since the 1920s yet was not available for purchase until 1953. A further characteristic of the Reinhart Collection is the inclusion of sculpture. Precious historical furnishings, tapestries, carpets and chandeliers create an ideal ambience for the presentation of the art works. The house «Am Römerholz» is, as a whole, a work of art – Oskar Reinhart, the «non-artist» had «a lofty appreciation of art».[16]

In 1922 Oskar Reinhart noted in his diary that he wanted «to serve mankind with his expertise and his possessions».[17] Reinhart was not only a collector, but also a patron of the arts: Artist friends Karl Hofer, Wilfried Buchmann, Hermann Haller, Alexandre Blanchet, Hermann Hubacher and Hans Sturzenegger all profited from his generosity. With the exception of the Expressionist Hofer, they are closer to the artistic tendencies of the nineteenth century than to the avant-garde of our century.

Oskar Reinhart's patronage not only embraced artist friends but also, in the broadest sense, society. His art appreciation was placed at the service of various delegations which included the Federal Art Commission and the Gottfried Keller Foundation. On several occasions his collection was shown in public exhibitions, for the first time in 1932 at the Kunsthalle in Basle. On this occasion, the University of Basle bestowed upon him the honorary degree «Doctor honoris causa» in recognition of his cultural achievements. Additional presentations followed, 1933 in Winterthur, 1935 in Lucerne, 1939 in Berne and 1940 in Zurich. At the opening of the exhibition in Berne, Oskar Reinhart remarked: «Even if one is the legal owner of such works, in a broader sense they are public property, and their owner can consider himself to be only a legal guardian».[18]

The following anecdote is typical of the somewhat reserved collector who loathed any hullabaloo about his person: the gallery was open to the public, by appointment, on Thursday afternoons. Those who came out of pure curiosity were liable to become the object of one of Oskar Reinhart's practical jokes. On such occasions he would appear in butler's livery and apologize for the absence of the collector. He would then sit back and enjoy the remarks made freely in the «butler's» presence. These tales later became a source of fun to him and his friends.

As early as 1930, Oskar Reinhart informed the city council of Winterthur of his intention to establish a foundation with a substantial part of his collection, making it permanently accessible to the public in a separate museum. Crises and years of war detained the realization of this plan.

Oskar Reinhart and Albert Fritschi,
hanging pictures at «Römerholz»

However, on January 21, 1951, following the reconstruction of the
former secondary school, the important Neoclassicistic edifice of the new
museum could be opened. The «Oskar Reinhart Foundation» includes
approximately 600 works of German, Austrian and Swiss art, from the
eighteenth to the early twentieth century. To mention only one main area,
the group of northern German Romantic painters with Philipp-Otto
Runge, Caspar David Friedrich and Georg Friedrich Kersting is of international significance.

In accordance with Oskar Reinhart's testament, the remaining private collection at «Römerholz» was to be handed over to the public. In
1958 he bequeathed the collection, together with the villa and park, to the
Swiss Confederation.

Oskar Reinhart died on September 16, 1965, shortly after his eight-
ieth birthday. Five years later, his villa was opened as a museum. Despite
the transformation of a private residence into a public gallery, much of
the personal atmosphere has been retained. The inspired path through
Western art begins with *The Annunciation* of about 1420, by a master of
the upper Rhine, and leads up to our century with an early Picasso. «Römerholz» is an oasis within the hectic business of art in which the carrou-
sel of exhibitions spins ever faster.

[16] OSKAR REINHART, letter to Theodor
Reinhart, London, 21 November 1907,
AORC.
[17] OSKAR REINHART, journal entry of
1922, AORC.
[18] OSKAR REINHART, speech on the occasion of the exhibition opening «Sammlung Oskar Reinhart» at the Museum of
Fine Arts in Berne, 16 December 1939,
AORC.

German and Swiss Painting
Late Gothic and Renaissance

The small panel of about 1420 by a master of the upper Rhine represents not only *The Annunciation,* but also a segment of reality with which the artist was familiar. The wondrous event does not take place before a background of gold, symbolic of eternity, but within the domestic

Master of an upper Rhine workshop
(Active the first quarter of the
15th century)
The Annunciation. c. 1420
Distemper on panel. 18.5 × 14.8 cm
Purchased 1927

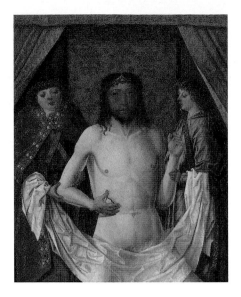

confines of a Gothic chamber. The walls, door, beamed ceiling and bullioned glass windows, the bed and receptacles on the wall-shelf, as well as the jug, potted plant and casket on the floor are portrayed with the same sense of intimacy as are the holy figures. A harmony between figures and space is imparted by the colouration. All the colours used to portray Mary and her chamber are repeated in the figure of the angel: On his wings the luminous blue of Mary's dress, for his garment the radiant red of the curtain, on his inner wings, the dazzling white of the book on the bed, the towel and descending dove. The empirical perception of space, which calls to mind the influence of Italian Trecento painting, and the naive joy with which the artist includes his own everyday surroundings in the biblical message are only a few characteristics of this predecessor of Konrad Witz. The small panel belongs to a group of closely related works which were produced in the region of the upper Rhine in the first quarter of the fifteenth century.

Master of a Salzburg or a Constance workshop (Active the second half of the 15th century)
Christ as Man of Sorrows. c. 1470–1480
Distemper on panel. 41.5 × 33 cm
Purchased 1938

Matthias Grünewald (1470–1528)
Mourning Woman with Clenched Hands
c. 1515
Black chalk on grey tinted paper
41 × 30 cm
Purchased 1926

The unknown master, who created the panel *Christ as Man of Sorrows* of about 1470–80, came under the influence of Michael Pacher's late style. Moreover, there exist stylistic correlations with the workshops of Salzburg and Constance. Supported by two angels draped in liturgical garments, Christ indicates the wounds inflicted on him during the crucifixion. In keeping with the type of pietà with angels which was widespread in Germany, the Man of Sorrows crowned with thorns is represented as having risen from the dead. He is not only the sufferer, but also the Redeemer who is triumphant over death.

MATTHIAS GRÜNEWALD is, beside Dürer, Altdorfer, the younger Holbein and Cranach the Elder, the most eminent German painter of his epoch. Among the few drawings by him which have been preserved, the *Mourning Woman with Clenched Hands* holds a dominant position. All of Grünewald's ingenuity is concentrated in this drawing, produced about 1515: His nervous, expressive style turns each line into a current of energy; the dramatic manner in which the artist handles both light and composition. The mental agony of this figure is emphasized by the convoluted, snake-like strands of hair falling over the face and shoulders, and by the agitated folds of the dress which are wrapped stiflingly around the arms and body. The torment is further expressed by the painfully twisted head, the hands clasped claw-like in despair, the lips opened to let out a cry and the squinting eyes. This study, no doubt drawn from a model, was used later by the artist for the portrayal of Mary Magdalene on the crucifixion corpus of the *Isenheimer Altarpiece* (Musée d'Unterlinden, Colmar).

On the altar antependium from eastern Switzerland, a traditional representation of *Saint Anne, the Virgin and Child with Saints Christopher, Stephen, Basil and Lawrence* is set into Late Gothic ornamental foliage, animated by nature studies and images of phantasy. Meadow flowers, birds tending their nests and squirrels cracking nuts enliven the scene, just as does the mermaid at the feet of Saint Christopher. The colourful wool embroidery, which formerly embellished an altar support, bears the date 1511.

Eastern Switzerland
Saint Anne, the Virgin and Child with Saints Christopher, Stephen, Basil and Lawrence
1511
Altar antependium. Wool embroidery
103 × 250 cm
Purchased 1931

17

Lukas Cranach the Elder (1472–1553)
Portrait of Johannes Cuspinian. 1502
Oil on limewood. 60 × 45 cm
Purchased 1925

The marriage portraits of *Johannes Cuspinian* and his wife *Anna Putsch*, painted 1502 in Vienna by LUKAS CRANACH THE ELDER, are major exponents of the German Renaissance. Preserved fragments of a heraldic shield of alliance on the back of Cuspinian's portrait made it possible to

identify the portrayed. Johannes Spiessheimer (Latin, Cuspinian), born 1473 in Schweinfurt, moved to Vienna in 1492 where, in December 1493, he was handed the poet's laurel wreath by Maximilian I. Together with this imperial distinction, Cuspinian was granted permission to hold lec-

Lukas Cranach the Elder (1472–1553)
Portrait of Anna Putsch. 1502
Oil on limewood. 60 × 45 cm
Purchased 1925

tures on poetics at the university. In 1494, he decided to become a physician. The emperor elevated him to the office of sovereign superintendent at the University of Vienna in 1501. Along with Konrad Celtis, Cuspinian soon occupied a leading position among the humanists of Vienna. His marriage with the approximately seventeen year old Anna, daughter of the imperial treasurer, Ulrich Putsch, was the occasion of Cranach's diptych.

In his standard work on the diptych, Dieter Koepplin points out that the landscape in this double portrait was given a new status as compared with Italian and Netherlandish prototypes: «In no other painting has the relationship between those who are portrayed and the landscape been so clearly established. [...] Above all, the landscape is not a mere attribute but the environment in which Cuspinian and his wife lived.»[19] There is something extraordinary in this landscape. A large number of small human figures and birds, a dog and a rabbit, a shining star above Cuspinian and flaming fire are elements of hidden pictorial symbolism. The artist not only captured the appearance of the portrayed at the time of their marriage, but also provided information about Cuspinian's philosophical and religious ideals. In accordance with neo-Platonic thought, Cranach disguised «the divine mysteries», which Cuspinian had requested he depict, with mathematical symbols and «poetic images» (Marsilio Ficino).[20]

A tiny figure close to Cuspinian provides a first clue to understanding the painting's complex symbolism which can be referred to only briefly here. The lyre, bow and raven identify the figure as Apollo. In a poem of 1501, Cuspinian implied proudly that Apollo had endowed him with his ability to compose and to heal. The nine women in the landscape, in connection with Apollo, can be interpreted as muses. An allusion to Christian baptism – the women washing and bathing – gives expression to a life that is pure and close to nature, the latter being a prerequisite for proximity to God. The supernaturally bright star in a clear blue sky, at which the scholar gazes, refers to God. «Cuspinian's heavenward glance includes both an orientation to Christ [...] and a readiness (therefore capacity) for greater insight.»[21] To the Christian humanist, knowledge, represented by the book he is holding, only had purpose «if one did not lose sight of the highest truth.»[22] In contrast to the star shining in the day sky, a preying owl stands for a demonic element of darkness. The owl, as wrong-doer and sinner beneath the divine light, should, according to Prudentius, admonish the Christian to transform his life into one of purity as conferred by baptism in the waters of Jordan. Water and fire, both present in the background, are elements of purification. However, other levels of meaning are also addressed. In the portrait of Anna Putsch, fire, like the parrot, is primarily a symbol of love. The little white dog and the rabbit it follows designate conjugal faithfulness and fertility, while the white carnation in Anna's right hand stands for virginity. Despite countless overlying symbols which are mutually elucidative, the portrait diptychon never loses its mysterious aura.

In contrast to the hidden symbolism of Cranach, the *Portrait of an English Lady,* executed around 1533–36 by HANS HOLBEIN THE YOUNGER, appears explicitly candid. Unlike the splendid settings in his portraits of richly clad members at court, the painter attains a subtlety of psycholog-

[19] DIETER KOEPPLIN, *Cranachs Ehebildnis des Johannes Cuspinian von 1502. Seine christlich-humanistische Bedeutung,* Basel 1973, p. 80.
[20] MARSILIO FICINO, quoted from: D. Koepplin, op. cit., p. 87.
[21] D. KOEPPLIN, op. cit., p. 164.
[22] D. KOEPPLIN, op. cit., p. 181.

Hans Holbein the Younger
(1497/98–1543)
Portrait of an English Lady. c. 1533–1536
Resin distemper on oak. 29.8 × 24.8 cm
Purchased 1934

ical expression in this portrait by keeping artistic media to a minimum. The young, modestly dressed woman in three-quarter profile, seated on a simple wooden bench against a neutral background, is completely self-absorbed, as demonstrated by her pose, expression and gesture; this inner quiet is reinforced by the handling of light, which casts almost no shadows, sharpness of contour and reduced colouration; the angular pearl-studded border of her headdress, set with a medallion, serves to intensify the softly modelled flesh colour of the oval face. The small dimple in the chin, together with the alert eyes and lips almost ready to smile interrupt and emphasize the rigidity of the pictorial arrangement.

Italian and Spanish Painting
Fourteenth to Nineteenth Century

Painted by a Florentine master about 1380, the *Coronation of the Virgin* shows a transition from Gothic to Renaissance. Traditional elements, such as the gold grounding, strict symmetrical arrangement and symbolic proportion of the figures, are combined with a corporeality, unusual for the time, which emerges beneath the richly coloured, non-schematically designed drapery. Added to this is a naturalistic accuracy of detail which is especially evident in the reproduction of the musical instruments. Christ and Mary sit enthroned, elevated beneath a baldachin held by two angels. Christ carefully places the crown on Mary's head. Two kneeling angels perform music at her feet, while Peter and John the Baptist on her right and Paul and Jacob the Elder on her left are in attendance. The well preserved panel, which originally ended in a pointed arch at the top, can be attributed to NICCOLÒ DI PIETRO GERINI because of stylistic characteristics. The artist was active in Florence from 1368 to 1415. A coronation of Mary by this master in the Montreal Museum of Fine Arts has much in common with our painting: Characteristic features, such as the way in which a pattern is embossed into nimbi and the ornamentation of Mary's gown, whose decorative motif disregards the plastic modelling of the drapery folds, are to a large extent identical in both panels.

A central theme in the work of JACOPO BASSANO is the *Adoration of the Shepherds* (p. 24). Their elemental bewilderment, their spontaneous reaction to the miracle – expressed through consternation, humility and a willingness to share – gave Bassano direct access to the Holy Family. His shepherds do not come from Arcadia. Marked by hard agricultural labour, these men are not types but individuals like those whom the artist would have seen as he worked daily in the countryside of Bassano. And yet, they form one family, together with Mary, Joseph and the Infant Jesus. Realistic elements of the landscape call to mind distinctive aspects of the hills surrounding Bassano. On the other hand, the ruins occupied by the Holy Family are detailed reminders of Dürer. This combination of precisely rendered reality and classical motifs copied from graphic models is typical of Bassano.

Our night scene was painted around 1565. The main source of light is the star of Bethlehem whose rays fall on the sleeping Infant Jesus. The supernatural brightness of the star together with actual light being kindled on the lower right by a young shepherd, and the cool, silvery tones of the setting sun form a triad lending the dark figures a visionary glow. Manneristic reminiscences of Parmigianino, who influenced

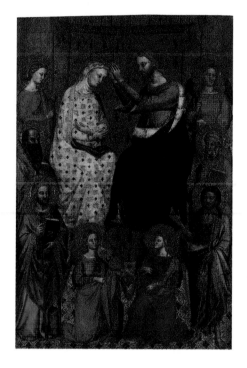

Niccolò di Pietro Gerini
(Active 1368–1415)
The Coronation of the Virgin. c. 1380
Distemper on panel. 75 × 49 cm
Purchased 1922

Jacopo Bassano (c. 1515–1592)
The Adoration of the Shepherds. c. 1565
Oil on canvas. 103 × 152 cm
Purchased 1928

Jacopo Tintoretto (1518–1594)
Portrait of Girolamo Grimani. c. 1565
Oil on canvas. 114 × 95 cm
Purchased 1922

Francesco Guardi (1712–1793)
Venice, Schiavoni Embankment
c. 1780–1790
Oil on canvas. 34 × 40.5 cm
Purchased 1912

Bassano's early works, are still evident in the shepherds' twisted bodies. Yet, all stereotypes have been overcome. Realism – the kneeling herdsman turns his dirty feet to the spectator – already anticipates the work of Caravaggio.

Derived from the same period as Bassano's *Adoration of the Shepherds* is a portrait attributed to JACOPO TINTORETTO which probably shows *Girolamo Grimani* at the Vatican as papal nuncio of the Venetian Republic. Admittedly, the poor state of the painting makes it difficult to attribute it to Tintoretto with certainty. If in fact the portrait is of the influential Grimani who died in 1570 – the fortress of Sant'Angelo in the background may uphold this identification –, then it seems plausible that Tintoretto did not leave this important assignment to his workshop but executed it, at least partially, himself. The masterful sketchy treatment of the robe and section of cityscape display not only the master's touch, but also the «impressionistic» qualities which Oskar Reinhart particularly valued in the old masters.

FRANCESCO GUARDI's late work *Venice, Schiavoni Embankment* (c. 1780–1790) is not a «vedute» in the original sense. The broad lagoon, enlivened by gondolas and barges, the dim light and misty veil over the surface of the water obstruct the view of Venice's main attraction, the Doge's Palace, accentuated by the bell tower of San Marco. Against a stormy sky, the illuminated city skyline of sombre hue appears like a vision. In this picture of atmospheric disintegration, the «Serenissima» is dreamlike rather than realistic. A mood of floating melancholy diffuses and the Baroque sense of transience finds a last sublime expression.

El Greco (c. 1541–1614)
Half-Length Portrait of a Cardinal. c. 1600
Oil on canvas. 74 × 51 cm
Purchased 1924

EL GRECO's *Half-Length Portrait of a Cardinal,* of about 1600, makes the spectator shrink back involuntarily. Not only the severity of the piercing gaze and hardness of the facial features, but also the violet and white of the gown, cape and collar, metallic colours in the cold light, place the figure at a psychological distance that is barely surmountable, despite the physical proximity. One is reminded of the dead commander whom Don Giovanni bade to a midnight repast. Captivating power radiates from the cardinal. Expositors have seen the horror of the Spanish Inquisition during the Counter Reformation embodied in him: It is difficult to decide whether the Wintethur painting is a preliminary study for the full-length portrait in the Metropolitan Museum of Art (New York) or a partial replica by the artist. Without a doubt, the same person is portrayed. The question as to the identity of the cardinal remains unanswered. He was thought to be Fernando Niño de Guevara who acted as the Grand Inquisitor in Toledo from 1599 to 1601; more recently, the powerful cardinal and Grand Inquisitor, Bernardo de Sandoval y Rojas, present in Toledo in 1600, has been taken into consideration.

Francisco de Goya (1746–1828)
The Laundresses. 1780
Oil on canvas. 86.5 × 59 cm
Purchased 1955

FRANCISCO DE GOYA is represented in the Reinhart Collection by six works from each of his creative phases, with two tapestry designs, two still lifes and two portraits. Goya worked for the Santa Barbara Carpet Manufactory in Madrid from 1775 to 1792. In 1780 he completed eleven designs for a series of tapestries for the antechamber to the bedroom of the Prince of Asturia in the El Pardo Palace. *Laundresses* belongs to this series. The oil sketch is accepted as being the original scheme for the full-scale cartoon (today in the Prado, Madrid) from which the tapestry weavers worked. In accordance with its decorative purpose, the composition consists of large areas of contrasting colours. It is not astonishing that the protagonists of these series of pictures were mostly «majos» and «majas». They belonged to the lowest stratum of eighteenth century Spanish society. One must remember that the Spanish aristocracy took pleasure in «plebeyismo» attire and in imitating the manners of the lower classes. Goya was aware of the contradiction in this courtly attitude. He was not making fun of the laundresses at work, rather the heartfelt solidarity of the resting women presented him with an image of primordial life.

Francisco de Goya (1746–1828)
Still Life with Fruit, Bottles and Bread
c. 1808–1812
Oil on canvas. 45 × 63 cm
Purchased 1937

Goya created a series of still lifes between 1808 and 1812. Whereas *Still Life with Fruit, Bottles and Bread* lies completely within the tradition of Spanish «bodegones», iconographically as well as in its composition and tonality, the radical artistic expression of *Still Life with Salmon* goes beyond the boundaries of this category. The three slabs of salmon, being neither allegorical nor anecdotal, lie in the glaring light on a grey table against a flat, black background. They are, in their matter-of-factness, neither more nor less than «nature morte»: still life. There is no abundance to suggest the wealth of God's creation; no concept of vanitas warns about redemption in the hereafter. The bestiality and brutality of the French-Spanish War, as recorded by Goya in the *Desastres de la Guerra* graphic series, is compressed, symbolically, into *Still Life with Salmon*. As Werner Hofmann wrote about Goya: «Nobody experienced the period of the Revolution more deeply and painfully, nobody gained from this experience a more powerful mastery of form and more puzzling spheres of meaning.»[23]

Francisco de Goya (1746–1828)
Still Life with Salmon. c. 1808–1812
Oil on canvas. 45 × 62 cm
Purchased 1937

Francisco de Goya (1746–1828)
Portrait of José Pio de Molina. c. 1827/28
Oil on canvas. 60.5 × 50 cm
Date of purchase unknown

Goya passed away in Bordeaux on April 16, 1828 at the age of eighty-two. One of his last paintings, the *Portrait of José Pio de Molina,* shows the friend who gave shelter to Goya, a victim of political persecution. In official portraits, the former court painter revealed the vacuity of aristocratic society with a «bravura» in depicting lavish apparel. In portraits of his friends, on the other hand, he sought to fathom out the individuality of his model by a reserved use of colour. It is not only that which remains unfinished or implied which is responsible for the unbreachable distance between the portrayed and the spectator, but also the singular, pale light in the picture. Goya painted this portrait with an awareness of his own future death.

[23] WERNER HOFMANN, *Goya und die Kunst um 1800,* in: Goya. Das Zeitalter der Revolutionen. 1789–1830, exhib. cat. Kunsthalle Hamburg 1980, p. 21.

Netherlandish Painting and Drawing
Fifteenth to Seventeenth Century

GEERTGEN TOT SINT JANS died at an early age. As his surname indicates, «With the brothers of Saint John», he worked in the Monastery of Saint John in Harlem, painting the *Adoration of the Magi* around 1480. Despite modelling his works on Flemish prototypes, particularly on the *Monforte Altarpiece* (Staatliche Museen Preussischer Kulturbesitz, Berlin) by Hugo van der Goes, Geertgen's creativity enabled him to develop the adapted composition beyond the ritualized schema. The child-like naturalness of the Infant Jesus lets an expression of naive tenderness shine through the faces and postures of the adults. Two of the Magi, one of whom is clearly oriental with his almond-shaped eyes, are shown kneeling and bareheaded, while the young Moor in splendid attire stands aloof. It may be that the three Magi represent the three continents known at that time, Europe, Asia and Africa, as well as the three ages of man. In the ruin where the Holy Family has found refuge, the decaying synagogue may be regarded as symbolizing triumph over the old faith through Christ's birth. The retinue of the Magi in the mid-ground of the painting relates the main event in Bethlehem to an imaginary Jerusalem in the distant landscape; on the left, the portal arch discloses a view of a village square where contemporary Flemish life unfolds in naturalistic surroundings.

GERARD DAVID, like Geertgen, was disposed to consult prototypes. However, these artists did not merely repeat that which they borrowed but relied on their personal sensitivity to create something new. Both instilled the landscape with a distinctive realism and futuristic expression. There is proof that David was in Bruges after 1484 and became the leading painter there after the death of Hans Memling. Two of his works are found at «Römerholz»: a *Crucifixion* and a *Pietà* (c. 1490). David formulated the «pièta» theme several times; the rendering at «Römerholz» derives from a panel in the Johnson Collection in Philadelphia. Unmentioned in the Bible, the mourning of Mary over her Son Jesus is rooted in fourteenth century mysticism. The devotional image is freed from the narrative context and is intended to make a direct appeal to the spectator; the silent moment of mourning after the removal of Christ's body from the cross, before it is laid in the tomb, focusses on Mother and Son. That this theme is referred to as «pièta» coincides with the liturgy of Good Friday whose prayers follow the stations of the cross; for this reason the descent from the cross and mourning took place during vespers in the late afternoon. The *Mourning* is an event because of the sublime spiritualization of pain expressed by Mary's restrained facial features and the mel-

Geertgen tot Sint Jans
(c. 1460/65 – before 1495)
The Adoration of the Magi. c. 1480
Distemper on oak. 135 × 101 cm
Purchased 1923

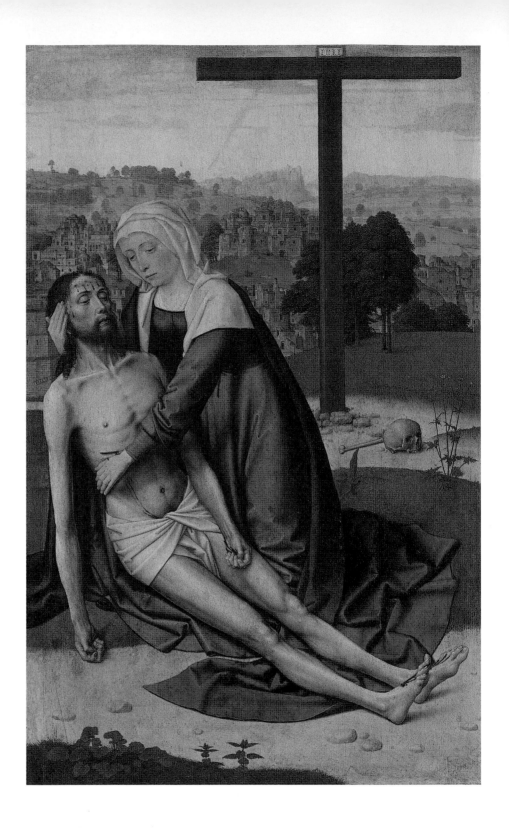

Gerard David (c. 1460–1523)
Pietà. c. 1490
Distemper on oak. 80 × 51.5 cm
Purchased 1931

ancholic atmosphere of the countryside. The composition of David's painting was influenced by Dieric Bouts and Rogier van der Weyden.

Produced in 1496, the sensitive *Portrait of Philip the Handsome*, attributed to the MASTER OF SAINT GILES, shows the ruler at the age of about eighteen years. His facial expression characterizes the young man

and suggests introspection rather than a desire for power and representation. The artist has accentuated his fine facial features, the play of his delicate hands and the golden sheen of his shoulder-length hair. It is conceivable that those who commissioned the painting wished to have this gentleness emphasized. The portrait may have been a gift for Johanna of Aragon, Philip's wife-to-be. He was born in Bruges in 1478, the son of Maximilian I and Mary of Burgundy. Already at the age of sixteen, he undertook command of the Netherlands which he governed with the skill of a statesman. In 1504 he became King of Castille and Leon. Even though he died at the young age of twenty-eight, he was an important link in the Habsburg dynasty: Through his marriage to Johanna, Spain came under Habsburg dominion; his son, Karl V, would make world history as emperor during the Reformation era.

A striking likeness of early Netherlandish sixteenth century painting is the *Portrait of a Man at the Age of Fifty-One* by QUENTIN MASSYS. His rendering of the facial features is absolutely true to nature; not the slightest flaw escaped the painter. The artist also captured, to a high degree, the personal expression which reveals the soul of his model. The man confronts his vis-à-vis with a furtive glance, evidence of ambivalent reserve and timidity. This contradictory effect is emphasized by the peculiar fall of light which, on the one hand, gives the face an almost tactile plasticity and, on the other, confounds the spatial situation by luminous dark shadows. Psychologically penetrating, the person does not give his identity away: The note in his hands merely imparts to posterity his age and the information that, in the year 1509, he had undertaken a journey to Jerusalem: «Etas mea 51 dum scriberetur 1.5.0.9. fui in terra sancta.»

Master of Saint Giles
(Active c. 1500)
Portrait of Philip the Handsome. c. 1496
Distemper on oak panel. 30.5 × 21.5 cm
Purchased 1933

Quentin Massys (c. 1466–1530)
Portrait of a Man at the Age of Fifty-One
c. 1510–1512
Distemper and resin paint on panel
48 × 33.5 cm
Purchased 1924

Only very little is known about the life and work of PIETER HUYS who painted *Saint Christopher*. Two major precursors shaped this artist: Hieronymous Bosch and Pieter Bruegel the Elder. Oskar Reinhart acquired the qualitative panel believing it to be the work of Bosch himself. However, doubts raised by research about this attribution were confirmed when the painting was cleaned and the signature «P. Hujis» was brought to light. Although Huys is certainly speaking Bosch's language in this picture, he is not lacking fantasy, adding hybrid creatures of his own to his predecessor's repository of devils and demons; his too is the effective thematic combination of Saint Christopher with the tempters and torturers of Saint Anthony.

Pieter Huys (1519–1584)
Saint Christopher. c. 1540–1560
Distemper on oak. 34 × 43 cm
Purchased 1923

The most important Netherlandish artist of the sixteenth century is PIETER BRUEGEL THE ELDER. As a humanist born into a period of radical political and religious turmoil, he granted traditional subjects a completely new kind of expression. His *Adoration of the Magi in the Snow* of 1567 differs fundamentally from all earlier depictions of the Nativity. «This painting is of exceptional art historical significance for two reasons: Firstly, it introduces a new type of winter scene into western painting, and secondly, it secularizes the old subject of the Epiphany in a hitherto unknown manner.» (Rudolf Koella).[24] By comparing this version with Geertgen's treatment of the same topic, also found in «Römerholz», it becomes clear that Bruegel's conception of the adoration of the Magi is something very new. The realistic rendering of the village in the background, the most trivial aspect of the painting has, in this work, been

[24] RUDOLF KOELLA, *Sammlung Oskar Reinhart Am Römerholz, Winterthur*, Zurich 1975, p. 58.

34

given a dominant position. Geertgen may cautiously have allowed some of his experience of daily life to find expression in the religious painting. Bruegel, however, let his Magi find the manger in a typical, anonymous village such as could be found in his Flemish homeland. There is no star to show them the way through the snowstorm, and none of the villagers let the miraculous happening disturb their daily life. The kings are weary. They have been searching for a long time. The way which lies behind them and has led them to the manger follows the diagonal of the painting. To the contrary, the spectator's glance is led past the spot of the divine happening in the lower left-hand corner until it comes to rest on the hustle and bustle of village life: Bruegel's message may have been a reminder not to lose sight of the right path in a period of religious reorientation.

Pieter Bruegel the Elder
(c. 1525/30–1569)
The Adoration of the Magi in the Snow. 1567
Oil on panel. 35 × 55 cm
Purchased 1930

35

Rembrandt Harmensz van Rijn
(1606–1669)
The Twelve Year Old Jesus in the Temple
c. 1642
Pen and bistre wash, heightened with
white, on paper. 22 × 29.5 cm
Date of purchase unknown

Willem Drost (c. 1630 – after 1680)
Manoah's Sacrifice. 1650–1660
Pen and bistre wash, heightened with
white, on paper. 19 × 28 cm
Purchased 1922

The attribution of a portrait and two drawings to REMBRANDT can now
be maintained with certainty only in the case of the *Twelve Year Old Jesus in
the Temple* (c. 1642). It is not a preparatory study, but rather an autonomous drawing, a collectors' item, even though it appears to be very
sketchy. In depicting the interior of the temple, the artist has obviously
been inspired by contemporary synagogues in Amsterdam. Not only the
rhythmic grouping of numerous figures into lively groups, but especially
the play of light in the dark room are extraordinary. Rembrandt lends the
scene a pictorial effect of magical expressiveness by the use of wash shad-
ing and white highlighting.

The important pen and ink drawing, *Manoah's Sacrifice,* and the re-
spective oil painting in the Staatliche Kunstsammlungen of Dresden have
meanwhile been identified as works of Rembrandt's pupil, WILLEM
DROST, who executed them between 1650 and 1660.

Aert de Gelder was Rembrandt's last significant pupil. He remained true to the late style of his master, uninfluenced by the classicism of his contemporaries. It was especially in his later works with the reduction of colour tonalities, pasty application of paint and his imaginative interpretations of historical themes that he achieved independence as a painter. The large-scale *Jacob's Dream* was painted by Aert de Gelder between 1690 and 1700 and has been slightly cut down on the right and left sides. The picture does not illustrate anecdotally the theme of the dream itself, the ladder leading to heaven, but rather the youthful dreamer himself, watched over by an angel, is represented with pictorial simplicity.

Aert de Gelder (1645−1727)
Jacob's Dream. c. 1690−1700
Oil on canvas. 172 × 117.5 cm
Date of purchase unknown

Philips Koninck (1619–1688)
Landscape with Town on Hillside. 1651
Oil on canvas. 62 × 86 cm
Purchased 1924

PHILIPS KONINCK'S speciality as landscapist were compositions of panoramic breadth. Like the universal scenes of the elder Bruegel and his followers, these compositions display splendid, majestic vistas from an elevated viewpoint; their natural, overall effect may disguise the fact that the careful combination of numerous motifs took place in the artist's studio and were based on an exact observation of nature. With his bright palette, bold manner of painting and contrapuntal consonance of earth and sky, he made a considerable contribution to Dutch landscape painting. When it comes to colour tonality and dramatization of light, *Landscape with Town on Hillside* confirms Rembrandt's influence on Koninck's early work.

AERT VAN DER NEER gives preference to broad river landscapes with a low horizon. The surface of the water, fading away into the depth of the painting, is always the central motif, the focal point usually lying

right above the river. The representation of the atmosphere is intensified by van der Neer's predilection for special impressionistic light effects. He was particularly fascinated by moonlight and, as in our *Winter Landscape with Ice Skaters* (c. 1655–1660), the magic of the setting sun. The surface of the frozen river was of interest to van der Neer, not only as a shining mirror reflecting the phenomena of light, but also as a place of many divers human activities. No other Netherlandish painter after Hendrick Avercamp has described in so much detail the attraction of the ice for the people as did van der Neer. Everyone romps on the frozen river: The peasant farmers from the huts on the right and left banks as well as distinguished citizens of the town in the background. Alongside idlers playing «kolf» (a kind of hockey) or enjoying themselves sleigh-riding and strolling, workers transporting kegs on sleds are also to be seen.

Aert van der Neer (1603/04–1677)
Winter Landscape with Ice Skaters
c. 1655–1660
Oil on canvas. 70 × 84.5 cm
Purchased 1923

The oil sketch for the second painting of an eight part cycle on Decius Mus, *Decius Mus Consults the Haruspicians* (1617), is a grandiose example of PETER PAUL RUBENS' artistic ingenuity for transforming historic scenes into works of art. In 1616, the artist was commissioned by the aristocratic circle of Genova to design cartoons for a tapestry cycle on the self-sacrifice of the Roman consul, Decius Mus, which led to his death. In the tradition of classical antiquity, Decius Mus was considered an «exemplum virtutis». Rubens himself outlined periods of this virtuous life in a series of eight original oil sketches from which, with the help of assistants, he completed the large cartoons which can be seen today in the collections of the Prince of Liechtenstein in Vaduz. These large-scale paintings were used as patterns for the execution of the wall hangings.

The heroic and self-sacrificing act of Decius Mus during the Latin War (340–338 B.C.) has been handed down by Livius: The Roman commanders-in-chief, the consuls, Titus Manlius and Decius Mus, saw themselves confronted by an enemy who was, by far, superior in strength. The decision came about as the result of a vision. In a dream, both consuls beheld a colossus who prophesied to them «that from one battle array the commander and from the other the army would be indebted to the divine spirits of death and to mother earth. Should the commander of one of the sides doom his enemy's legions and himself to death, his people and army would be granted victory.»[25] At the onset of the battle against the Latins, Titus Manlius and Decius Mus, each prepared to give up his life for Rome, ordered that steers be slaughtered as offerings. The priestly seer or «haruspex» discovered the decisive omen in the entrails of the steer which Decius Mus had sacrificed.

Rubens portrayed the reactions to the fateful prophecy: how the sudden realization befalls Decius Mus, the emotion reflected in the faces of Titus Manlius and the priest and fright and confusion in the faces of the standard-bearers and the retinue. While the steer of Titus Manlius is forcibly held back by the «victimarii», servants accountable for killing the animals, the steer of Decius Mus lies slain on the ground. At the feet of Decius Mus, a golden bowl full of blood is an allusion to his own immolation, and the candle, blown out by the boy beside the altar, signifies the extinction of his life.

Rubens consciously planned his composition to compete with Raphael's *Saint Paul at Lystra* (Victoria & Albert Museum, London), one of the famous cartoons on the Acts of the Apostles. As an expert on antiquity, Rubens demonstratively corrected the minor historical errors made by Raphael. In the «Römerholz» sketch, Rubens has captured the essence of the composition, which concentrates wholly on the hero, with rapid brushstrokes. The spectator is, as it were, an eye-witness to the painting's genesis. Content and form are in perfect accord. Rubens did not let this topic draw him to superficial hero-worship. Rather he portrayed tragic fate and human greatness with empathy. Full of admiration, Jacob Burckhardt wrote in 1898: «In these images lives a powerful and unsought sense of the Romans' magnitude which, for example, David and his followers, with all of their pathos, never achieved.»[26]

[25] LIVIUS, quoted from: Reinhold Baumstark, Peter Paul Rubens. Tod und Sieg des römischen Konsuls Decius Mus, Vaduz 1988, p. 25.
[26] JACOB BURCKHARDT, *Erinnerungen aus Rubens* [1884/93, first ed. 1898], in: J.B.-Gesamtausgabe, vol. 13, Basle 1934, p. 472.

Peter Paul Rubens (1577–1640)
Decius Mus Consults the Haruspicians. 1617
Oil on oak. 74 × 104 cm
Purchased 1954

French Painting and Drawing
Seventeenth and Eighteenth Centuries

Rome was the adopted home of NICOLAS POUSSIN, a contemporary of Rubens, Rembrandt, Bernini and Velázquez. Through continuous intellectual encounters with antiquity and exposure to Raphael, the Roman Baroque and Venetian appreciation of colour, he developed his own classical conception of art. With his «maniera magnifica» of well-balanced compositions, he brought a forceful, new expression of timeless validity to the traditional themes of mythology, religion and history. According to an anecdote passed on in 1672 by his first biographer, Gian Pietro Bellori, the «peintre-philosophe» reached first for a book rather than a brush when a topic for a painting was suggested to him.

The theme of *The Holy Family* (p. 44) inspired Poussin – similar to Raphael – to a series of impressive paintings, beginning around 1632 with the important example at «Römerholz». Contrary to the Gospel according to St. Matthew in which only brief mention is made of the flight of the Holy Family into Egypt, the apocryphal writings tell of many wonderful events. Among them it is related how cherubs delight the divine Child with flowers and fruit when the Family stops to rest. Poussin captures this moment of relief which follows the exertions and fears of the journey. The scene is portrayed in an ancient temple ruin, a truly classical setting. The composition is one of great harmony, despite the agitated liveliness of the cherubs; their movements follow the direction indicated by the Child Jesus and the bodies of Mary and Joseph who lean slightly towards Him. This cheerful scene is replete with allusions: One is directed at contemporary theatre – the cherub lifts the red curtain –, others to theological matters: The garland of flowers above the head of the Christ Child refers to the crown of thorns. In accepting the apple, the symbol of the Fall, Jesus takes upon himself the original sin of mankind. The old world order is in ruins, as symbolized by the crumbling columns of the Roman temple, whereas the living tree behind the Child Jesus stands for the vitality of a new era.

CLAUDE LORRAIN is the second outstanding French painter of the seventeenth century. Like Poussin he took up residence in Rome. Beginning with Netherlandish models, impressed and challenged by Poussin and Domenichino, he painted landscapes in which his intensive study of nature and of Roman ruins are concentrated into a visionary perception of antique and biblical states of harmony. The restoration of *Landscape with Hagar and the Angel* (p. 45) in 1992 left no doubt that it had been painted by Claude Lorrain. Radiant beams of light from the setting sun il-

luminate the scene. The antithetical composition is rhythmically structured by groups of trees, temple ruins, ranges of gently rolling hills and sheets of water. The landscape unfolds in depth from left to right, along a path on which a shepherd drives his herds, whereas the action moves in the opposite direction. The angel, arm outstretched towards the far left, shows Hagar Abraham's house to which the outcast maiden should return. In contrast to the rules of history painting and showing a lack of fidelity to the biblical text, Claude's subject grows out of the elegiac effect of classical ideal and the enchanting harmony between nature and man; it is this which makes his paintings of special interest to us today.

Claude Lorrain (1600–1682)
Landscape with Hagar and the Angel. 1654
Oil on canvas. 99 × 131.5 cm
Purchased 1951

Nicolas Poussin (1594–1665)
The Holy Family. c. 1632
Oil on canvas. 87 × 66 cm
Purchased 1925

In his genre painting and still lifes, JEAN-BAPTISTE-SIMÉON CHARDIN achieved a naturalness and spontaneity that removed him far from academic artificiality, thus enabling him to develop an uncommon sensibility for the materiality of simple objects and their changing appearance in light. French still life painting reached its first climax in Chardin's work. His painting of *The House of Cards* (c. 1735) combines the timelessness of a still life with the immediacy of genre painting. It shows a youth who is carefully building a small, fragile house of playing cards. The soft, warm light which causes the mellow colours to glow corresponds both to his youthfulness and to his dedication to the game. He is unaware of the symbolic meaning of his activity, namely that the house of cards, which can collapse at any moment and, as a symbol of vanitas, alludes to the precariousness and transience of all human endeavour; the inconstancy of fate in affairs of the heart is especially emphasized, inasmuch as the next card the youth will put down is the ace of hearts. A copperplate engraving, based on the first example of this subject, provides the viewer with an appropriate epigram:

«Vous vous moquez à tort de cet adolescent
Et de son inutil ouvrage
Prest à tomber au premier vent.
Barbons dans l'âge même où l'on doit être sage
Souvent il sort de vos serveaux
De plus ridicules châteaux.»[27]

(«Wrongfully, you are amused by the young boy
And by his futile work
That will collapse with the first breeze.
Grown grey with old age, a time when one should be wise,
Your heads still bring forth
Even more laughable castles in the air.»)

The still lifes *Crystal Bowl and Fruit* and *Water Glass and Fruit* are counterparts. Chardin painted them in 1759, the year in which they were exhibited at the Parisian Salon. Chardin's deceptive imitation of nature is what enthused his contemporaries most of all. In his Salon commentary, Denis Diderot, referring to an anecdote of an artist of antiquity, wrote: «The peach and grapes whet the appetite and tempt the hands.»[28] Both small-sized still lifes are masterpieces of Chardin's intimate art. Various compositional triangles join the objects into rhythmic lively groups which are related to each other. And what atmospheric appeal there is in the magic of the light! It was Diderot who praised the artistic quality of Chardin's still life painting: «This man understands harmony of colours and their reflections. Oh, Chardin, it is not white, red and black pigment that you are crushing on your palette; it is the very substance of the object, it is air and light which you take with the tip of your brush and put onto the canvas.»[29]

[27] The copper engraving is reproduced in: PHILIP CONISBEE, *Chardin*, Oxford 1985, p. 140.
[28] DENIS DIDEROT, *Salon de 1759*, in: Diderot. Salons, vol. 1: 1759, 1761, 1763, ed. by Jean Seznec and Jean Adhémar, Oxford ²1975, p. 66.
[29] DENIS DIDEROT, *Salon de 1763*, in: J. Seznec and J. Adhémar, op. cit., p. 222.

Jean-Baptiste-Siméon Chardin
(1699–1779)
The House of Cards. c. 1735
Oil on canvas. 61.5 × 64 cm
Purchased 1922

Jean-Baptiste-Siméon Chardin
(1699–1779)
Still Life with Crystal Bowl and Fruit. 1759
Oil on canvas. 37 × 45.5 cm
Date of purchase unknown

Jean-Baptiste-Siméon Chardin
(1699–1779)
Still Life with Water Glass and Fruit. 1759
Oil on canvas. 36 × 45 cm
Date of purchase unknown

François Boucher (1703–1770)
Reclining Nude. c. 1745–1750
Charcoal, heightened with white,
on green tinted paper. 26 × 39 cm
Purchased 1926

FRANÇOIS BOUCHER and JEAN-HONORÉ FRAGONARD are eighteenth-century French painters «par excellence». In their light-hearted manner, the agility of the brush and drawing implement erases the customary boundary between sketch and painting. Next to the finished work, the equally valid «alla prima» brushwork now emerged, so that Diderot could pose the once unthinkable question: Why does a beautiful sketch have more appeal than a beautiful painting?

While Boucher's *Reclining Nude* (c. 1745–1750), a drawing and study, achieves the pictorial effect of a painting, in Fragonard's spirited and loosely painted «capricco» *Satyr and Bacchantines* (c. 1773–1774), bold rapid brushstrokes take precedence over contouring and modelling. Fragonard treated mythology as freely as he did the painting of the work. It was merely a pretext for giving free rein to his imagination. Even when he illustrated a literary text, he relied solely on fantasy. He was especially captivated by Cervante's «Don Quixote». Of the numerous drawings which he completed on this subject during the 1780s, «Römerholz» possesses three sheets: *Don Quixote Taken Unawares while Reading, Don Quixote Fighting Against an Armature, Don Quixote's Arrival at the Inn.*

Jean-Honoré Fragonard (1732–1806)
Don Quixote Taken Unawares while Reading
1780–1790
Black chalk and bistre wash on paper
41 × 27.5 cm
Purchased 1933

Jean-Honoré Fragonard (1732–1806)
Don Quixote Fighting Against an Armature
1780–1790
Black chalk and bistre wash on paper
41.5 × 27.5 cm
Purchased 1933

Jean-Honoré Fragonard (1732–1806)
Satyr and Bacchantines. c. 1773–1774
Oil on panel. 32.5 × 41 cm
Date of purchase unknown

Neoclassicism and Romanticism in France

The antipodal pairs David / Géricault and Delacroix / Ingres clearly illustrate the polarity between Neoclassicism and Romanticism in the «Römerholz» Collection. The confrontation of the works of these artists on the long walls of the main gallery bring about a meeting of the vibrant passion of Romanticism with the coolness of Neoclassicism. In this antagonism between «fire and ice», Oskar Reinhart included the principal

Jacques-Louis David (1748–1825)
Portrait of Pauline Jeanin. c. 1810–1813
Oil on canvas. 73 × 60 cm
Purchased 1949

forerunners of both styles: The pictorial baroque of Rubens alludes to the romantic «rubenistes», while Poussin's principle of linearity is continued by the classical «poussinistes».

Between 1810 and 1813, JACQUES-LOUIS DAVID portrayed his wife, his twin daughters Pauline and Emilie as well as their husbands, both officers under Napoleon who had been raised to nobility. The *Portrait of Pauline Jeanin* (p. 51) gives a frontal view of the young woman in «empire» dress. This very position candidly highlights the fact that neither her facial features nor her neck are without flaw. David conveyed an extremely realistic impression of his daughter. Her slightly mocking, pouting smile seems to be true-to-life. The playful ease with which the paint has been sketchily applied corresponds to the spontaneity of the facial traits and, indeed, seems to be its cause. Only when it came to family portraits did David distance himself from formal, well composed Neoclassicism. The *Portrait of Pauline Jeanin* occupies a prominent and exceptional position among his late works: it attests to the importance which David attached to colour accords as a compositional means after 1810.

A strange and frightening realm breaks into portrait-painting with THÉODORE GÉRICAULT's renderings of the mentally ill, one of which, *Monomaniac Obsessed with Military Command,* is found in the Reinhart Collection. In the winter of 1863, Louis Viardot discovered a package in a dusty attic in Baden-Baden which contained a roll of five canvases, Géricault's portraits of the insane. The text which Viardot published in 1864 is the first known document about this series of portraits. The latest research questions their source. Viardot assumed that Géricault had been commissioned by Dr. Georget, the Parisian physician for the mentally ill, to paint portraits of some patients for scientific study. Certain is that the series of paintings was completed between 1819 and 1822, at the beginning of Georget's career. For this reason, it seems more likely that his teacher, Dr. Esquirol, who was committed to institutional reform, had commissioned the portraits. According to Esquirol's new theory, the monomaniac is deranged in one respect only and otherwise behaves quite sensibly. With this view he revoked the conventional demarcation between reason and insanity.

This blurring of distinct boundaries was characteristic of Géricault's romantic temperament, just as it was for Goya. Géricault's insane figures are in contemporary dress. Contrary to conventional depictions of social outcasts which fascinated the Spanish court of the seventeenth century, Géricault avoided everything grotesque. Herein one might see an enlightened reference to the possibility of cure and rehabilitation of the patient. However, the thin line between reason and the outbreak of destructive, irrational life-forces becomes all the more evident in the portrait of a *Monomaniac Obsessed with Military Command,* inasmuch as the uniformed madman, with his piercing and at the same time evasive gaze, is painted with the aloofness of a clinical report. From this, one can conclude that Géricault took the deranged man seriously, as an individual, and found nothing about his condition which he needed to conceal. Géricault, being a romantic, may have been so fascinated by insanity, because he believed that this imbalance was accompanied by a more strongly articulated vitality and depth of perception, comparable to that of artistic genius.

Théodore Géricault (1791–1824)
Monomaniac Obsessed with Military Command. c. 1819–1822
Oil on canvas. 81 × 65 cm
Purchased before 1936

A second important work by Géricault in the Reinhart Collection is the small *Portrait of General Le Tellier on his Deathbed* of 1818. This general did not die in battle. Stricken with grief over the death of his wife, Le Tellier shot himself in bed; there his friends, Louis Bro and Géricault, found him a few moments later. General Bro gave an account of this event in his memoires: «He lay in his bed on white sheets, clothed in a white shirt; he had wrapped one of his wife's scarves around his head, his fist still clasped her handkerchief, and between his clenched teeth was one of her rings. A pistol lay on his bed, still warm. Just a few minutes before his friends arrived, he had shot himself in the heart.»[30] Géricault imparted a heroic dignity to the banality of death in bed by referring back to David's historical portrayals of the dead.

Théodore Géricault (1791–1824)
Portrait of General Le Tellier on his Deathbed. 1818
Oil on canvas. 24 × 32 cm
Purchased 1953

[30] LOUIS BRO, *Mémoires du général Bro (1796–1844)*, edited by Baron H. Bro de Comères, Paris 1914, p. 176.
[31] JEAN-AUGUSTE-DOMINIQUE INGRES, *Du dessin*, quoted from: Ingres, raconté par lui-même et par ses amis, vol. 1, Geneva 1947, p. 56.

The Neoclassicism of JEAN-AUGUSTE-DOMINIQUE INGRES is a vital continuation of the late academic style of his teacher, Jacques-Louis David. The outlined drawing which distinguishes his compositions lends itself to confined, static forms. Even in private portraits, his unconditional veneration of antiquity can be felt. In the *Portrait of Delphine Ingres-Ramel,* profane reality is elevated to timeless classic: her pose is of aristocratic affectation, her youthful complexion pure like marble, her attire and jewels of flawless splendour. Her gaze indicates a temperate disposition. Good two years after the death of his first wife, Ingres married Delphine Ramel who was younger than he by a generation. Courting had not been a simple matter; there were, after all, three rivals, one of whom was extremely wealthy and had to be outstripped. The wedding took place on April 15,

Jean-Auguste-Dominique Ingres
(1780–1867)
Portrait of Delphine Ingres-Ramel. 1859
Oil on canvas. 63 × 50 cm
Purchased 1924

Jean-Auguste-Dominique Ingres
(1780–1867)
Portrait of Antoine Thomeguex. c. 1822
Pencil, heightened with white, on paper
32 × 22.9 cm
Purchased 1935

1852. The marriage was perfectly harmonious. The painting of 1859 shows Madame Ingres at the age of fifty-one. Even though the materiality of every detail is captured with absolute precision, the painting nevertheless takes on a restrained liveliness because of its treatment of light and harmony of colour.

The *Portrait of Antoine Thomeguex* is evidence of the poignant clarity and pictorial effect which Ingres was able to achieve in his drawings. It is quite obvious that Ingres elevated the drawing to an independent work of art: «Drawing is the integrity of art»[31]. The portrait originated around 1822 in Florence. In his hometown of Geneva, Thomeguex, a watchmaker by profession, made a name for himself as a composer of song and as a member of the city council. His son, Pyrame, ran a straw hat factory and was a friend of Ingres. Thomeguex attended his son's wedding in 1822 in Florence where Ingres painted his portrait: The dignified pose in three-quarter attitude of the Genevan city councilman is sketched with a few strokes; the sixty year old poet's finely modelled face and features, full of character, reveal a mischievious heartiness.

Following the early death of Géricault, EUGÈNE DELACROIX reluctantly became the leading spokesman of French Romanticism. Traditionalist and revolutionary, he held not only Rubens and Rembrandt in high esteem, but also Italian painting of the past, as attested to by innumerable copies from all of his creative periods. He did not, however, find the crucial impulse he needed in the countries of these artists, but rather on the savage soil of North Africa. Like Ingres, he took his themes from literature, the Bible and history, but his goal was not a realistic, illustrative representation of them. Rather, in making his emotional response the theme of his paintings, he remained true to his motto: «I myself am the subject.» In his turbulent and passionate paintings, showing scenes of battle, murder and betrayal, suffering and death, the most important moments of extreme inner tension reach their culmination.

The span of Delacroix's artistic career is represented at «Römerholz». The earliest work of 1826 shows the dramatic *Scene from the Greek War of Independence*. In relation to the restorative political circumstances in Europe, the battle of liberation of the oppressed Greek people was an explosive event. Delacroix relied on his imagination to create this painting which portrays a nameless battlefield, full of gunsmoke, on which no heroes are to be found. The composition concentrates for the most part on three figures. It is not only this, but also the bright colours which blend the painting into a whole. The influence of Constable is still felt in the open spaces of the landscape in which the gaze becomes lost.

Eugène Delacroix (1798–1863)
Scene from the Greek War of Independence
1826
Oil on canvas. 65 × 81 cm
Purchased 1921

Eugène Delacroix (1798–1863)
Tasso in the House of the Insane. 1839
Oil on canvas. 60 × 50 cm
Purchased 1919

Delacroix, like Géricault, took up the subject of insanity, but in relation
to a literary source: Lord Byron's Ode «Lament to Tasso» was an event
which led Delacroix to study intensively the work and life of the Late
Renaissance Italian poet. No doubt he saw in Torquato Tasso a fel-
low-sufferer, interned as he was in the asylum in Ferrara. The poet sits
languidly on his divan. He has lost interest in his manuscripts. He has
become an object of derision for the insane, and his genius has been de-
stroyed by society's intolerance. It is obvious that the topic of this painting is related to the life of the artist: When Delacroix first took up the
subject of *Tasso in the House of the Insane,* the editor of «Journal des Ar-
tistes» called for his internment in the asylum of Charenton. The second
version of 1839 differs from the first by renouncing the portrayal of lux-
urious costumes and embellishment with anecdotal details. It concentrates
on the isolation of the pensive poet and on the renewal of the traditional
motif of melancholy which plays an important role in Delacroix's œuvre.

Eugène Delacroix (1798–1863)
Ophelia's Death. 1844
Oil on canvas. 55 × 64 cm
Purchased 1960

[32] EUGÈNE DELACROIX, letter to Jean-Baptiste Pierret, 25 January 1832, in: *Correspondance générale d'Eugène Delacroix,* ed. by André Joubin, vol. 1: 1804– 1837, p. 307.

The Romantics, with their pugnacious break from academic tradition, found in Shakespeare's anti-classical literature one of their guiding stars. Delacroix, alongside Henry Fuseli, is the great interpreter of Shakespeare among artists. He painted three versions of *Ophelia's Death,* a scene from Hamlet, the second of which (1844), the most subtle, is at «Römerholz». Delacroix has chosen an event which is not performed on stage, focussing on the short moment just before destiny takes its incessant course: in the next instant, Ophelia will let loose of the branch and sink into the torrent. Despite the loosly applied paint with its subtle effect, the monochromatic colouring dramatically underscores the melancholy of the scene.

In 1832, Delacroix accompanied Count Charles de Mornay, ambassador of Louis-Philippe, to the Sultan of Morocco. The oriental, adventurous world of North Africa became the embodiment of primitive and vital energy for the artist. He felt himself transported back to ancient Greece. He drew unceasingly, at times even on horseback. «At the moment, I seem to myself to be like someone who sees things in a dream and is afraid that he will not be able to remember them»[32], he noted in Tanger. His paintings were clearly influenced by the exotic world and glaring light of the south, where colours are pure and lustrous. By the end of his life, Delacroix's painting had changed; it became freer, more colourful and dynamic. *Moroccan Artillery Practice* of 1847, *Samson and Delilah* of about 1850 and *Fighting Lion and Tiger* of 1854 illustrate this impressively.

Moroccan Artillery Practice is a glowing tribute to the wildness of the headstrong galloping Arabian stallions. The painter restricted himself to a narrow section so that only the rump and back hooves of a dashing horse are recognizable on the far left of the picture. This daring, rhythmical composition of groups of riders is colouristically intensified by complementary contrasts: pure red in the foreground finds a quiet counterpart in the green of the landscape.

Eugène Delacroix (1798–1863)
Moroccan Artillery Practice. 1847
Oil on canvas. 66 × 82 cm
Purchased 1936

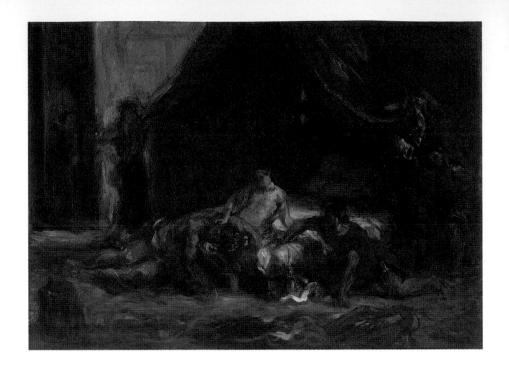

Eugène Delacroix (1798–1863)
Samson and Delilah. c. 1850
Oil on paper, mounted on panel
41 × 56.5 cm
Purchased 1936

The betrayal of love is the actual subject of the sketch-like painting, *Samson and Delilah*. Delacroix communicated the instant just before the decisive moment. Devotedly, the one dedicated to God sleeps, his head on the lap of his beloved to whom he had revealed the source of his strength. Already the Philistines, to whom Delilah had sold the secret, have responded to her signal and forced their way into the chamber. The one with the shears slithers like a snake to cut off Samson's seven locks and thereby rob him of his Herculean powers. The creative passion and empathy of the artist manifest themselves in the vehemence of the sketchy brushstroke.

Delacroix painted *Fighting Lion and Tiger* «with enthusiasm», as he noted in his diary on October 12, 1854[33]. This scene, deserted by man, combines an admiration for Rubens with reminiscences of Morocco and reaches a climax in the brutal strength of the animalistic. It was of little interest to the artist that lion and tiger never confront each other in the wild. It was for him a question of the symbolic content: the fight between equal opponents will reach its end only with the death of one of them.

Tobias and the Angel of 1863, the year of the artist's death, is one of Delacroix's last works. Compared with his early achievement it becomes clear how his painting evolved from romantic gloom into orphic light. The influence of wall-painting which simplifies the line and monumentalizes the figures is expressed here, even in the small format of an easel picture. In the same year, Delacroix's entry in his diary, which also serves as a legacy, clarifies the lyrical and soft accords of colour: «The first merit of a painting is to be a feast for the eyes.»[34]

[33] EUGÈNE DELACROIX, journal entry, 12 October 1854, in: E. D., *Journal 1822–1863*, ed. by André Joubin, Paris 1980, p. 483.
[34] EUGÈNE DELACROIX, journal entry, 22 June 1863, in: A. Joubin, op. cit., p. 808.

Eugène Delacroix (1798–1863)
Fighting Lion and Tiger. 1854
Oil on canvas. 46.5 × 56 cm
Purchased 1923

Eugène Delacroix (1798–1863)
Tobias and the Angel. 1863
Oil on canvas. 40.5 × 32.5 cm
Purchased 1923

Early Impressionism

Long before Impressionism, there were artists at the beginning of the nineteenth century who elevated the phenomenon of nature, rather than the actions of man, to the main concern of their artistic process. The Englishman, JOHN CONSTABLE, is an independent opponent to Neoclassicism and an important precursor to the landscapists of early French Impressionism. For his picture *Branch Hill Pond, Hampstead* in 1825, he reproduced a section of landscape to the north of London which has, in the interim, become a part of the vast city. The persons found in the hilly expanse are observed reality, just as the landscape and atmospheric impression which dominate their momentary appearance. The region of Hampstead is not at all spectacular, neither unusually picturesque nor classically eminent. One must look carefully in order to perceive its quiet charms: the gentle succession of hills and dales, accents set by shrubs and hedges, areas of grass and patches of sand. This section of nature becomes an event through the effect of light. A thunderstorm is gathering in the cloudy sky. While solitary tracts of land are still lit by the sun, others lie in

John Constable (1776–1837)
Branch Hill Pond, Hampstead. 1825
Oil on canvas. 60 × 77 cm
Purchased 1932

shadows; changing light causes the same shade of colour to vary constantly in intensity and refraction. Delacroix was among the first to recognize this quality. Twenty years after his first encounter with the Englishman, Delacroix still cited in his diary excerpts of a conversation with the admired landscapist: «Constable says that the green of his willows is not imitable, because he relies on innumerable tones of green for his composition. The lack of intensity and liveliness in the greenery of mundane landscapists is a result of using one single tone. This comment about the green of the willows applies just as much to all other shades of colour.»[35]

Two almost identical versions of *Branch Hill Pond, Hampstead* exist and were produced in quick succession. Constable painted this second example, found at «Römerholz», for the French art dealer, Claude Schroth. The artist accounted for the popularity of his landscapes in France in a letter to his friend, John Fisher, in 1824: «They [the French] are struck with their vivacity and freshness, things unknown to their own pictures. The truth is, they study (and they are very laborious students) pictures only; and as Northcote says, 'They know as little of nature as a hackney-coach horse does of a pasture.' In fact, it is worse, they make painful studies of individual articles, leaves, rocks, stones, etc., singly; so that they look cut out, without belonging to the whole, and they neglect the look of nature altogether, under its various changes.»[36]

Camille Corot (1796–1875)
Stony Chestnut Wood. c. 1830–1835
Oil on canvas. 54 × 84 cm
Purchased 1923

Camille Corot (1796–1875)
Bridge near Mantes. c. 1855–1860
Oil on canvas. 23.5 × 35 cm
Purchased 1923

A first look at CAMILLE COROT's early work *Stony Chestnut Wood* seems to prove that Constable was right. Nature is clearly structured even if Corot, unlike Claude Lorrain in his ideal *Landscape with Hagar and the Angel* (p. 45), skillfully hides the compositional framework. Whereas Claude uses the herd to accentuate the path following the diagonal into the far background, the path in Corot's picture disappears between boulders and trees. During his first Italian sojourn from 1825 to 1828, Corot painted his first Realistic landscape studies with sun-drenched colouration, in the clear light of the south. Until the late 1840s, he still portrayed his first-hand experiences of nature in keeping with the rules of traditional landscape painting. The composition and totality of the motif, not a partial view, are just as traditional as the precision with which details of the landscape and the genre-like figures are characterized. Alongside these classicistic tendencies, the dramatic shadows allude to Romantic influences. And yet this work, painted by Corot in the Auvergne around 1830–1835, is evidence of his sensitivity to the colourful manifestation of the landscape and his dedication to the «appearance of nature in all its changing moods».

A total of six landscapes at «Römerholz», three of which are singled out here, show Corot at the height of his artistic career: *Bridge near Mantes* (c. 1855–1860), *Château-Thierry* (c. 1855–1865) and *Dunkerque Fisher Port* (1873). These spontaneous segments of nature, displaying almost no order in the composition, portray the same motifs: the vast areas of sky, expansive bodies of water, trees, fields and meadows, a town silhouette or a bridge. Within these landscapes, the people going about their daily activities, without the artist taking much notice of them, are almost without significance: farmers, fishermen, washerwomen. These landscapes appeal to the spectator on an emotional level. The atmosphere casts a spell. The delicate ghost-like shapes of the objects lose their earthly gravity. The silvery mist lying over this world transforms everyday reality into melancholic and lyrical tones. In these insignificant details, Corot praises the still and powerful hand of nature.

[35] EUGÈNE DELACROIX, journal entry, 23 September 1846, in: E.D., *Journal 1822–1863*, ed. by André Joubin, Paris 1980, p. 881.
[36] JOHN CONSTABLE, letter to John Fisher, 17 December 1824, quoted from: C. R. Leslie, Memoirs of the Life of John Constable, Oxford ²1980, p. 134

Camille Corot (1796–1875)
Château-Thierry. c. 1855–1865
Oil on canvas. 38 × 55.5 cm
Purchased 1936

Corot's landscapes can be viewed as an illustration to Adalbert Stifter's preface to «Bunte Steine»: «The blowing of the wind, water trickling, grain growing, the surging of the sea, the sprouting of the earth, the gleaming of the sky, the shimmer of stars, all these I consider to be great; the splendidly approaching storm, lightning that rents houses apart, the storm which sets waves in motion, a mountain spewing forth fire, an earthquake that buries countries are not greater than the above phenomena; indeed, I consider them to be less, because they are only the effects of much higher laws.»[37]

Camille Corot (1796–1875)
Dunkerque Fisher Port. 1873
Oil on canvas. 40 × 55.5 cm
Purchased 1948

Camille Corot (1796–1875)
Girl Reading. c. 1855–1865
Oil on canvas. 46 × 38.5 cm
Purchased 1938

Corot let himself be guided by the immediacy of the momentary mood. What matters is the painterly revelation, the subjective impression. In this regard, like the painters of the Barbizon School with whom he was loosely bound, he is already an Impressionist. Nevertheless, in contrast to Monet, Sisley and Pissarro, the pictures begun outdoors were, according to his comprehensive vision, developed further in his studio into a nuance-rich harmony of colours and shapes.

Corot's figure painting too seldom gives expression to literary themes. His œuvre does not fit into the current categories of portrait, genre or history painting which were familiar to his contemporaries. His dreaming women never seek contact with the spectator. Rather, they are passive and introspective. Even the musical instruments and books which occupy them do not disclose their secrets. They appear to be dreaming about the soft, melancholy sounds as expressed by the landscape. And so they too are a transposition of lyrical sensation into painting. «May you be guided only by your heart» was Corot's motto for budding artists.[38]

[37] ADALBERT STIFTER, preface for *Bunte Steine* [1852], Munich 1951, p. 8.

[38] CAMILLE COROT, quoted from: Etienne Moreau-Nélaton, Corot raconté par lui-même, Paris 1924, p. 105.

[39] JEAN-FRANÇOIS MILLET, letter to Alfred Sensier, 1 Februar 1851, quoted from: Etienne Moreau-Nélaton, Millet raconté par lui-même, Paris 1921, pp. 90–91.

Camille Corot (1796–1875)
Young Woman with Mandolin. c. 1860–1870
Oil on canvas. 55 × 39.5 cm
Purchased before 1930

Camille Corot (1796–1875)
Italian Woman Playing a Mandolin
c. 1865–1870
Oil on canvas. 61 × 50 cm
Date of purchase unknown

Girl Reading (p. 67), despite her youth and tenderness, appears especially monumental, lost in her book before the vast landscape. Not only has Corot made the act of reading the topic of this painting, but also the contemplation of what has just been absorbed. The cool silvery tone of the landscape and the young reader's intense feelings seem to intermingle. A perfect harmony of colour accords prevails between sky, landscape and figure.

The *Young Woman with Mandolin,* wearing a classic, timeless garment, holds her head in her hands, a melancholic gesture. The mandolin is in her lap. She has interrupted her playing and listens wistfully to the fading tones.

On the other hand, the *Italian Woman Playing a Mandolin* is actively immersed in her performing. The timbre of the strings evokes yearning in both mandolin players; this is emphasized by their exotic clothes. This free representation of dress shows the extent to which Corot let himself be guided by the effect of colour; pattern and cloth are completely dissolved in painterly structures.

Jean-François Millet (1814–1875)
Apple Harvest. c. 1870
Oil on canvas. 73 × 60 cm
Purchased 1923

Jean-François Millet (1818–1875)
Reading Lesson with Mother and Child
c. 1855–1860
Black chalk, heightened with white,
on paper. 28.5 × 21 cm
Date of purchase unknown

JEAN-FRANÇOIS MILLET's early Impressionism lies between Corot and
Courbet. The harmony between intact countryside and its unspoilt inhab-
itants, praised by Millet in his representation of farmers and agricultural
labourers, sums up the quality of his art. He found his motifs in Barbizon,
fifty kilometers south of Paris, among a circle of like-minded landscapists
such as Théodore Rousseau, Jean-François Daubigny and others. *Apple
Harvest,* a late work of about 1870, links colouristically the motif of farmers' hard labour to an early impressionistic landscape. While Courbet in
his *Stone-Breakers* (p. 81) diagnosed, without illusion, the misery and want
of the country population cut off from industrial development, Millet saw
natural forms of life protected in this backwardness. He certainly saw
«the earnestness and difficulty of human existence» in the poor people
working the land, but also, as he wrote in the same letter of February 1,
1851, «genuine humanity and true poetry»[39].

French Realism

As far as HONORÉ DAUMIER was concerned, there was only one theme: mankind. In his comprehensive work of graphic prints, about 4000 lithographs and 1000 woodcuts, the artist did not restrict himself to portraiture and caricature when depicting his contemporaries. Daumier exposed their feelings, hopes, disappointments and, above all, their weaknesses. Intended for newspapers and periodicals, the lithographs' severe social criticism and political attacks were provocative to the extent of landing the young artist behind bars. The skillful line of his drawings and a pictorial language whose relevance is far-reaching, keep these politically engaged works topical.

Although a large collection of Daumier's graphic art is on display at the Oskar Reinhart Foundation, «Römerholz» offers a less renowned but artistically significant aspect of his œuvre. As well as watercolours and drawings, nine oil paintings from a total of about only 250 are on view. Daumier's love of experimentation in the medium of painting led to a disregard for the traditions of the studio with varying results. At the same

Honoré Daumier (1808–1879)
Children Bathing. c. 1855–1857
Oil on canvas/paper. 24.5 × 33 cm
Purchased 1936

Honoré Daumier (1808–1879)
The Fugitives. c. 1848–1855
Oil on canvas / paper. 38.5 × 68.5 cm
Purchased 1922

Honoré Daumier (1808–1879)
A Third Class Waiting Room. c. 1860
Black chalk and watercolour on paper
26.5 × 21 cm
Purchased 1927

Honoré Daumier (1808–1879)
A Third Class Carriage. c. 1865
Black chalk, pen and Indian ink,
watercolour, heightened with white,
on paper. 23 × 33 cm
Purchased 1923

time, on a private 'side-track', he anticipated and influenced many of the achievements of future generations, from Manet via Toulouse-Lautrec and van Gogh to the Fauves and German Expressionists.

Thematically, Daumier's painting is distinct from graphic art in proportion as it frees itself from the explicitness of the picture's content. This does not mean to say, however, that there is no reference to time. Hence, in *The Fugitives*, Daumier took up a recurring theme in the history of mankind. An endless flow of fugitives, extending beyond the limits of the pictorial field, drag themselves over a mountain pass. Naked or in rags, these people cannot be placed in a specific epoch. Only one thing is certain, they have not undertaken their journey voluntarily. Cast out, they flee from that which lies behind them. This picture, with its simple, lowly message, could stand for the fate of every refugee, from biblical history to the present day. Alert contemporaries of Daumier may also have seen a political message therein. Painted during a period of disillusionment and disappointment over France's development following the Revolution of 1848, the work may have awakened memories of the suppression of the Parisian workers' rebellion in June 1848 or the deportation of approximately 10 000 people which followed the national strike under Louis-Napoléon in 1851.

People en route is a recurrent motif throughout Daumier's work. A great novelty of the industrial age was the railway; this motif had, at first, been treated in lithographic series from an amusing point of view. From the mid 1850s, Daumier added a new and deeper dimension in drawings and oil paintings. With a sharp, socially critical eye, he observed the passengers in the compartments of the different classes. The comical situation of a mixed bag of travellers takes on new meaning by concentrating on the individual. In the prints *Third Class Carriage* and *A Third Class Waiting Room*, the occupants' position in life is impressively reported with a minimum of graphic elaboration. The journey together in a third class compartment relates the history of individual destinies with the history of a social class.

Don Quixote, relentlessly driven, could in no way be enticed to stay in one place. Daumier's interest in Cervantes' hero began in 1850 and increased during the late 1860s until the artist's death in 1879. From the first phase, «Römerholz» possesses the masterful charcoal drawing of *Don Quixote Somersaulting before Sancho Pansa* (p. 74). It shows the tragic figure of the knight, dressed only in a shirt, performing somersaults before his servant Sancho Pansa to convince him of his passion for Dulcinea. The laughable foolishness, almost anecdotal, is an exception to Daumier's confrontation with his hero. He nearly always portrays him as a lonely, isolated figure, erect and motionless as he passes through unknown

Honoré Daumier (1808–1879)
*Don Quixote Somersaulting before
Sancho Pansa.* c. 1850–1855
Charcoal on paper. 34.5 × 25 cm
Date of purchase unknown

wildernesses. In *Don Quixote and Sancho Pansa in the Mountains* (c. 1866–1868), the contrasting natures of the two men are especially emphasized: The tall, scrawny one with a curvature of the spine rides his miserable hack into an illusionary future, while the short fat man, slumped on his donkey, worriedly looks reality in the face. Brooding and down to earth, *Sancho Pansa beneath a Tree* (c. 1868–1870) becomes for once the main figure, whereas his master appears as a mere silhouette on the horizon. Daumier's representations of Don Quixote are not illustrations of the literary work. Rather, they are an expression of personal affinity. The French artist reflects his own role as an outsider, as an artistic commentator of social conditions, in the anachronistic Spanish knight.

Honoré Daumier (1808–1879)
Don Quixote and Sancho Pansa in the Mountains. c. 1866–1868
Oil on panel. 29.5 × 45 cm
Date of purchase unknown

Honoré Daumier (1808–1879)
Sancho Pansa beneath a Tree. c. 1868–1870
Oil on panel. 46 × 37 cm
Purchased 1925

Honoré Daumier (1808–1879)
A Counterargument. c. 1864
Charcoal, pen and Indian ink,
watercolour on paper. 22 × 33 cm
Date of purchase unknown

Honoré Daumier (1808–1879)
The Plea. c. 1867–1870
Black chalk, pen and Indian ink wash,
watercolour on paper. 23.5 × 28.5 cm
Purchased 1927

Honoré Daumier (1808–1879)
The Lawyers. c. 1865–1867
Black chalk and watercolour, heightened
with white gouache, on paper
15 × 23.5 cm
Purchased 1938

Honoré Daumier (1808–1879)
Return from Market. c. 1855–1857
Oil on canvas. 35 × 28 cm
Purchased 1936

Honoré Daumier (1808–1879)
Two Doctors and Death. c. 1857–1860
Black chalk, pen and Indian ink,
watercolour on paper. 32.5 × 28 cm
Purchased 1922

Don Quixote's escape into a fantasy world was probably fascinating to Daumier who questioned unceasingly the social norms and obligations of contemporary life. With a keen eye, Daumier put the ordinary, the typical, the commonplace and mediocre under a magnifying glass and commented caustically on what he saw. In addition, Daumier criticizes certain professions in particular. In the print *Two Doctors and Death*, two physicians are arguing theatrically about the correct diagnosis, while in the background Death is already carrying the patient out of the door. The biting cynicism about the doctors' false pride corresponds to that about the corrupt attorneys and judges who, in the prints *A Counterargument*, *The Plea* and *The Lawyers*, do not bring much honour to their professional standing. In contrast, the oil paintings *Children Bathing* (p. 71) and *Return from Market* describe everyday scenes and are free of all derision. Both were painted around 1855–1857 but represent different painterly conceptions. While the bathing scene still concentrates on the plasticity of the body in the traditional sense, the decorative play of pure areas of colour dominates in the painting of the horseman.

Honoré Daumier (1808–1879)
The Art Lovers. c. 1869
Pen and Indian ink, watercolour on
paper. 18 × 24 cm
Purchased 1948

Honoré Daumier (1808–1879)
Pierrot with Mandolin. c. 1869–1873
Oil on panel. 35 × 26.5 cm
Purchased 1928

The Art Lovers represent a contemplative side of Daumier's œuvre. Grasped by tranquil ardour, the men inspect a number of works of art. Their humble delight in these prints creates for them an ideal world of their own which nothing can mar. For once, Daumier does not make fun of this subject which he often treated with derision. Rather, he celebrates the type of collector of whom he would have liked to have seen more.

One of the last paintings in Daumier's œuvre, *Pierrot with Mandolin*, is one of his boldest works. The theme of the entertainer, as an allegory for the artist's own isolation, finds its freest expression in this late pictorial representation. In its sketchiness, evocative of Fragonard, contour, space and volume become unimportant; a fleeting, groping brush endeavours to grasp the image in the process of painting.

Gustave Courbet (1819–1877)
The Hammock. 1844
Oil on canvas. 70.5 × 97 cm
Purchased 1924

The comprehensive collection of ten works, beginning with *The Hammock* of 1844 and ending with *The Wave* of 1870, demonstrates the scope and development of Gustave Courbet's artistic work. The finely drawn young woman, asleep in the *Hammock*, has sculptured facial features and an artificial flesh tone; the blossoms and leaves of the rosebush and the surrounding trees are painted in minute detail. This work clearly reflects Neoclassicistic painting, the sleeping beauty calling to mind the «odalisques» of Ingres. Nevertheless, Courbet's Realism, with its essential characteristics, is already clearly established; typically enough, the work, entered by the artist in the 1845 Salon, was rejected by the jury. Draped as the young woman is in the hammock, swaying over a natural spring, it is clear that she is no longer a nymph: Not only are the allegorical requisites

Gustave Courbet (1819–1877)
Bather at a Stream. 1845
Oil on canvas. 88.5 × 68.5 cm
Purchased 1936

missing which would allude to the mythological sphere, but still more revealing and scandalous is her bourgeois attire – nymphs do not wear
socks! The idyll of the disrobed woman asleep undergoes a turn to the
prosaic. Although the figure is presented artistically in a light, wave-like
pose, the sagging hammock reveals the weight of the body it is support-
ing. Sleep may well transport the beauty into the realm of dreams, but in
her corpulence she remains mortal and real to the observer.

The triad of woman, spring and landscape becomes a leitmotiv in
Courbet's later œuvre. Hence, the naked *Bather at a Stream* can be interpreted as the personification of nature. She is one with the vegetation
which surrounds her like a niche, and her left arm seems to grow into the
branches. An almost tangible senuousness is achieved by the treatment of
light that leaves her face in shadow and particularly by the liveliness with
which the paint has been applied. The brushwork used for the *Bather*,
dated only a year after *The Hammock* but probably originating about
1860, eliminates any Neoclassicistic sense of drawing and treats the nude
body just as freely and as flowingly as the vegetation in the background.

80

The most famous work in the collection is the study of 1849 for the scandalous composition *The Stone-Breakers*. Painted over another work, it appears murky and not very spectacular at first sight. After the disappearance of the final composition in Dresden at the end of the Second World War, the «Römerholz» study has become its most important substitute. The labour of the two men who are breaking up stones and collecting them is endless and arduous. Tattered, dirty and stooping, they carry out their hard task. The image is free of pathos, the situation represented most soberly. Both men are faceless, their movements seem to have become torpid. There appears to be no escape from the dreariness of their existence, and even the sullied spot of sky in the upper right-hand corner removes any illusion.

The reactions which the picture released at the 1855 Salon, earning Courbet the reputation of «peinture socialiste» with friends and foes alike, might seem astonishing in view of the «Römerholz» study. These reactions are understandable only if one takes into account the fundamental difference between the study and the final painting: the format. The

Gustave Courbet (1819–1877)
The Stone-Breakers. 1849
Oil on canvas. 56 × 65 cm
Purchased 1923

Gustave Courbet (1819–1877)
Grape Harvest at Ornans. 1849
Oil on canvas. 71 × 97 cm
Purchased 1938

stone-breakers drew attention at the Salon, because they were almost life-size, thus making their presence felt. Miserably dressed and engaged in wearisome labour, these representatives of the working class laid claim to a format which was usually reserved for the heroic deeds of renowned personages. The artist who was on friendly terms with Proudhon, the philosophizing socialist, wanted, only indirectly, to make a political comment. His painting was not intended to be a vehicle for transmitting ideas; the sober, realistic depiction of the situation was political enough for him.

Grape Harvest at Ornans, a landscape painted in the same year as *The Stone-Breakers*, displays a subject which remains a constant element throughout Courbet's œuvre. It is the huge, free-standing tree, always filling at least half of the pictorial space which led to the concept «tree portraiture» in the literature on Courbet. The action in the picture, the grape harvest of the vintagers in the background, is of secondary importance. An exact observation of the light, especially as it appears on the crest of the tree, is worthy of attention. In *Flower Still Life* of about 1863, the light is also exalted to become the central theme. It is easy to understand that Courbet's painting of the 1860s was a model for the Impressionists Monet and Renoir.

The artist's exact observation of characteristic features reveals itself in the *Portrait of Gustave Mathieu* (1869). The businessman and part-time art dealer, who attained fame as an author of drinking aphorisms and satirical songs, was a friend of Courbet. His cynicism is hidden behind the earnest, nearly devastating stare. His is an intrusive face, dominant and obscure. In contrast to this executioner's gaze, an enormous corsage of roses in his lapel seems to divulge another side of this personality – qualities of the cavalier Mathieu.

The Wave, dated 1870, belongs to a series of dramatic depictions of waves which Courbet began in 1869 during his stay in Etretat and contin-

Gustave Courbet (1819–1877)
Flower Still Life. c. 1863
Oil on canvas. 65 × 54.5 cm
Purchased 1949

Gustave Courbet (1819–1877)
Portrait of Gustave Mathieu. 1869
Oil on canvas. 73 × 60 cm
Purchased 1963

ued until 1872. Since the artist was no longer able to travel to the seaside after the outbreak of the German-French war, it is certain that the picture in Winterthur was not painted on the spot. Yet even in this version, an archaic phenomenon of nature finds expression in the crushing force and threatening power of the rolling wave. The paint was, for the most part, applied rapidly and thickly with a palette knife and becomes transformed into foaming spray. If one recalls sweet and artificial pictures of waves, such as Cabanel's *Birth of Venus* (Musée d'Orsay, Paris), the reactions of the public to Courbet's massive breakers are amazing. They proved to be a great success at the Salon, thus showing how diverse and contradictory salon taste had become at the close of the Second Empire.

Gustave Courbet (1819–1877)
The Wave. 1870
Oil on canvas. 80.5 × 99.5 cm
Purchased 1925

Impressionism

The works of the inner circle of the Impressionist avant-garde, whose eight self-organized group exhibitions caused a great stir, are exhibited at «Römerholz». Whereas an important phase in the œuvre of Claude Monet, Alfred Sisley, Camille Pissarro and Edgar Degas is represented by a principal work of each of these artists, the thirteen paintings by Pierre-Auguste Renoir characterize the collection of Impressionist works as a whole. Reinhart was partial to sensuous, atmospheric Impressionism as embodied by Renoir. He was less interested in the notation of a mere process of perception which allowed painting to become an end in itself to an unknown degree.

PIERRE-AUGUSTE RENOIR never painted without a model. Unlike the consistent Impressionism of his friend Monet, his paintings were intended to be more than accurate reproductions of sensory impressions. Renoir's art contains a subjective response to that which is seen. Only in a few early, consciously experimental works such as *La Grenouillère* of 1869 (p. 87) does his brushstroke succumb to a rigorous disintegration of form. Renoir's search for the soft, rounded form, and his occasional confrontation with tradition separate him from the Impressionist landscape painters and shift him nearer to Manet and to Degas. His decisive rejection of Japonism – the adaptation and modification of motifs and characteristics of Japanese art – also grants him a special position among his French companions.

His earliest picture in the collection is *Calla Lily and Greenhouse Plants* (p. 86). The artist painted it in 1864 at the age of twenty-three, two years after he had given up his job in a porcelain workshop and enrolled in the Ecole des Beaux-Arts and at the Paris studio of the Swiss painter Charles Gleyre. Monet's *Still Life with Flowers* (Museum of Art, Cleveland) was completed in the same year and shows a comparable colouration and brushstroke. In contrast to Monet's elaborate flower arrangement, Renoir's composition seems to be more incidental. Pots and boxes of large and small flowers are scattered randomly on the floor. Even though the arrangement is intentional, the purposeful grouping gives the impression that one has come upon it by chance in a garden or a greenhouse. In actuality, the picture originated in the studio of Frédéric Bazille who, no doubt, was thus given the impulse for a very similar composition with flowers two years later. The brushwork is not yet Impressionistic. The precise reproduction of identifiable plants suggests the influence of Courbet's Realism. The accurately drawn calla lily dominates the foreground; behind it stand pots of tulips, lilac, blue cinerarias, pink pelargoniums, white hyacinths, white cineraria and, next to the calla in the front, a box of bell-flowers and two pots of sciripus grass. If one recalls the low ranking of still life within the academic tradition, well below historical painting, portraiture and landscape, then the extremely large format of this painting is astounding. Perhaps it was meant to be submitted to the Salon, certainly not as an avant-garde provocation but, with its perfect finish and representative format, as a masterpiece by the young painter.

Pierre-Auguste Renoir (1841–1919)
Calla Lily and Greenhouse Plants. 1864
Oil on canvas. 130 × 96 cm
Purchased 1927

In 1869, Renoir and Monet paid many visits to the Seine islet, La Grenouillère, between Chatou and Bougival and painted there side by side.
This popular meeting place consisted of a public bathing establishment
and a restaurant where dances were held. Both painters found here the
motifs they were looking for: colourful bathers, row-boats, trees and especially shimmering water in which everything was alluringly reflected.
Their pictures often show the same motif, documenting that both artists
had painted there simultaneously. Monet's chief interest was the study of
the phenomena of light on the water's surface which also assumes an important position in Renoir's *Grenouillère* in Winterthur. The technique of
horizontal rows of comma-like flecks of colour, boldly thrown, unmixed,
straight from the tube, certainly achieved such spontaneity as a result of
Monet's encouragement. Our example could be mistaken for one of his
works.

The carefree world represented in the *Grenouillère* paintings tends to
overshadow the difficult situation in which the two artists found themselves at that time. Monet wrote to Bazille in August of that year: «We
have had no bread, fire or light for the past eight days.»[40] Nevertheless,
they painted incessantly until Monet's painting materials ran out at the
end of August. These deprivations make doubly clear how uncompro-

Pierre-Auguste Renoir (1841–1919)
La Grenouillère. 1869
Oil on canvas. 65 × 92 cm
Purchased 1931

[40] CLAUDE MONET, letter to Frédéric Bazille, 9 August 1869, in: Daniel Wildenstein, Claude Monet. Biographie et catalogue raisonné, vol. 1: 1840–1881. Pein-
tures, Lausanne/Paris 1974, letter no. 50,
p. 426.

Pierre-Auguste Renoir (1841–1919)
Garden at Fontenay. 1874
Oil on canvas. 51 × 62 cm
Date of purchase unknown

mising the *Grenouillère* pictures are. They could not count on the goodwill of the public. Monet wrote again to his friend Frédéric Bazille that he was planning to use the plein air studies of Grenouillère to paint a large work for the Salon.[41] At that time, he must have considered these works to be more like studies, as opposed to his later appraisal of them which generally coincides with that of the present day. He was not yet aware of having discovered his own new style of painting. Moreover, self-assessment and experience would no doubt have shown him that this succint and sketchy manner of painting would not meet with the approval of the Salon jury. To be sure, neither Renoir nor Monet endeavoured to submit a *Grenouillère* landscape in the following year. Monet was completely eliminated by the jury; a *Bather* and an *Odalisque* by Renoir were accepted, the former reminiscent of Courbet, the latter a hommage to Delacroix.

Garden at Fontenay originated in 1874, the year of the first Impressionist exhibition. Its fragmentary, grid-like structure differs greatly from the technique of parallel commas of colour used in the *Grenouillère*. While the individual plants in the floral still life (p. 86) could be identified with ease, only the foxglove is recognizable in the flower beds which are composed succintly of flakey patches of colour. The garden in Fontenay-aux-Roses belonged to the couple Le Cœur, friends of Renoir. As suggested by Rudolf Koella, the two women dressed in black are almost certainly the lady of the house and her daughter. At the age of thirty-three, the painter fell in love with the sixteen year old Marie to the disapproval of her parents, an event which led to the end of the relationship. Therewith Renoir lost an important patron. All the same, he was better off than many of his friends. His nudes and portraits gradually won the approval of a public who rejected the innovative landscape painting. The opinion

of the day was expressed by Albert Wolff, art critic of the «Figaro», who saw in the «impression at which the Impressionists were aiming», nothing more than «a cat strutting about on the keys of a piano or a monkey which has gotten hold of a paint-box»[42].

Unruffled by current opinions, the Parisian customs officer, Victor Chocquet, found access to the art of the Impressionists. With limited means, he had acquired several works by Delacroix and believed to have found in Renoir a young painter who was carrying on the tradition of that painter. For this reason he requested Renoir to portray his wife in front of one of Delacroix's works. To be sure, Chocquet's highest admiration would be for Cézanne whom he met through Renoir and who was to portray him repeatedly just as Renoir had done. Whereas Cézanne characterized Chocquet as a robust personality, he appears gentle and of delicate constitution in Renoir's *Portrait of Victor Chocquet* of 1876. With finely placed brushstrokes and a differentiated, light tonality, Renoir tended to expose his sitter's spiritual qualities which he valued highly. Here too, however, the sensation of colour was fundamental: The painter did not hesitate to depict the hair of the seated man in iridescent yellow-green tones.

A year earlier, Renoir portrayed his *Milliner* in front of the same floral background. With this motif, he took up a topical theme of the avant-garde. The themes of many paintings by Manet and Degas were determined by a straight-forward, sober look behind the scenes, free of the tabus of genre-painting which disclosed the precarious situation of milliners, laundresses and ironers; these women were sometimes depicted as alcoholics. Indeed, Renoir's focus lay somewhere else. He was not concerned with the depiction of social problems, but rather with the col-

Pierre-Auguste Renoir (1841–1919)
Portrait of Victor Chocquet. 1876
Oil on canvas. 46 × 36 cm
Date of purchase unknown

Pierre-Auguste Renoir (1841–1919)
The Milliner. 1875
Oil on canvas. 59 × 49 cm
Purchased 1948

[41] CLAUDE MONET, letter to Frédéric Bazille, 25 September 1869, in: D. Wildenstein, op. cit., letter no. 53, p. 427.
[42] ALBERT WOLFF in: Figaro, March 1875, quoted from: Gustave Geffroy, Claude Monet. Sa vie, son œuvre, Paris 1924, vol. 1, chap. 8.

Pierre-Auguste Renoir (1841–1919)
Intimacy. 1878
Oil on canvas. 61.5 × 50.5 cm
Purchased 1923

ouristic transformation of a workaday scene. He turns his model, shown in strict profile, into an enchanting being, placing her in a world of flowers and bows, a reminder of life in the eighteenth century. As in the *Portrait of Victor Chocquet*, Renoir's manner of painting is especially delicate, almost becoming the very air itself.

Renoir's portraits of the 1870s are characterized both by an Impressionistic approach that is caught up in the stimuli of shades of colour and the play of light, and by a subjective moment, the painter's personal reaction to his model. This is especially clear in *Intimacy* of 1878. Two young women, before a backdrop of dense foliage, are immersed in sharing secrets. The women were Renoir's favourite models. Although the one facing us can be identified, it is not the realistic representation of her facial features which is of importance here. What strikes the eye is the reflexion of light and the ethereal, hazy colours, bringing to mind a wonderful bouquet of flowers or a peach in a still life. One can almost hear ringing laughter and whispering; the affectionate intimacy suggests what the subject of the conversation may be. The viewer almost believes that he is hiding behind a bush, eavesdropping.

Pierre-Auguste Renoir (1841–1919)
Sleeping Woman. 1897

Oil on canvas. 82 × 66 cm
Date of purchase unknown

Sleeping Woman (p. 91) represents the period that superseded Renoir's Neo-classicistic phase and, after 1900, led into his late style: The so-called mother-of-pearl period. No other conception could better characterize the central theme of the *Sleeping Woman*. It is flesh that breathes, flesh that gleams. The shimmering light dances on the well-rounded female body as if it were a pearl. Finely graduated brushstrokes of thinly applied colour form the full figure and, at the same time, lend it a weightless transparency. Even though the sleeping woman, arms behind her head, freely presents her body to the eye of the viewer, she does not seem to be expecting this intrusion. The same applies to her as to many female nudes of the 1890s: She is part goddess, part model, timeless, yet sensuously present. Sleep blurs the boundaries, surrounding her with an aura of enchantment. Realism in spite of idealism is revealed by Renoir's laconic comment: «The naked woman will rise from the salty surf or from her bed; her name will be Venus or Nini. One will find nothing better.»[43]

One of the most beautiful paintings of nudes of the years 1910–1920 is the painting *After the Bath*. With the progression of his severe physical suffering, the elderly painter was even more strongly attracted by themes full of life. Thus Andrée, a youthful, voluptuous model and servant who was to become the wife of his son Jean, is a characteristic female figure in his late works. Renoir's distressing loss of vitality found compensation not only in the motifs, but even moreso in the act of painting itself. The superior brushwork and the intensity with which he gave colour a meaning of its own demonstrate clearly in this painting the relationship between the late works of Renoir and the younger colourists like Bonnard.

Pierre-Auguste Renoir (1841–1919)
After the Bath. 1913
Oil on canvas. 100.5 × 81 cm
Purchased 1923

Painted just prior to the outbreak of the German-French War, *Barges on the Saint-Martin Canal* brought recognition to a fellow struggler among the Impressionists, ALFRED SISLEY. This painting and a second version of the same canal were accepted by the jury and exhibited at the Salon in 1870. This one was acquired by Edouard Manet shortly thereafter. In keeping with Impressionistic precepts, the scene is in no way an expression of social criticism despite its motifs: to the right of the canal, behind the trees, industrial and commercial buildings, to the left workers who are unloading barges. The sensation of colours and the play of light, as well as shadows and reflections are of central importance. Compared with Renoir's daring disintegration of form in *La Grenouillère*, Sisley's landscape, composed of carefully placed commas of colour, seems more cultivated. Seen at a distance, the loosely woven patches of colour in the foreground condense to give a strong impression of shimmering water.

Sisley had been encouraged to paint «en plein air» by Monet whom he had met for the first time, together with Renoir and Bazille, in Gleyre's studio. Common studies of landscapes in the surrounds of Barbizon were crucial. Although Sisley had managed to exhibit at the Salon at an early date, he did not experience success before his death in 1899. This as opposed to Renoir and Monet, both of whom enjoyed growing recognition from 1885 onwards.

Alfred Sisley (1839–1899)
Barges on the Saint-Martin Canal. 1870
Oil on canvas. 54.5 × 73 cm
Purchased 1923

43 PIERRE-AUGUSTE RENOIR, quoted from: Hans Graber, Auguste Renoir. Nach eigenen und fremden Zeugnissen, Basle 1943, p. 230.

Claude Monet (1840–1926)
River Seine with Ice-Floes. 1881
Oil on canvas. 60 × 99 cm
Purchased 1924

CLAUDE MONET's painting of *River Seine with Ice-Floes* of 1881 depicts in cold tones surging ice-floes on a branch of the Seine. Presenting a view of the Iles de Moisson near Vétheuil, it belongs to a series of winter landscapes produced from 1880 to 1882, following the death of Monet's wife, Camille. The immediate cause of his preoccupation with this theme, as Monet repeatedly explained in his letters, was the great thaw of ice in 1880 which had been accompanied by violent storms and floods. There is, however, little evidence of these eruptive forces in our version. It emanates a deep sense of solitude and melancholy, isolation and detachment from the world. Yet, almost concurrently, its heaviness and coldness seem to disperse into air as a result of the rapid brushwork – an effect that is reinforced by the ghostly verticals of the poplars.

It is customary to view Impressionist works of art at due distance; one should, however, also examine *River Seine with Ice-Floes* at close range. The paint was applied very thinly; this is especially evident in the water area where the grey ground coat is still visible, showing how relatively few brushstrokes can convey poetic charm. The contrast between the horizontally applied patches of colour for the ice-floes and the vertical reflections of the poplars in the water anticipate an important characteristic of Monet's series of *Water-Lilies* in Giverny.

CAMILLE PISSARRO was the integral figure within the heterogeneous group of Impressionists. On his initiative, controversial painters like his friend Cézanne were invited to participate in their joint exhibitions; it was Pissarro who acted as mediator between the two groups which had begun to crystallize around Monet and Degas. He was also the only one who took part in all eight of the Impressionist exhibitions, and, despite his lack of financial means, he agreed to forgo all participation in the Salon.

The Hermitage at Pontoise was painted in 1874, the year of the first exhibition. Pissarro had close connections with the town of Pontoise which lies to the north-west of Paris. He resided there from 1866 to 1868 and from 1872 to 1882. The motifs to which the artist was attracted were not spectacular: simple farmhouses, gardens, insignificant crossroads and hilly countryside. One suspects almost nothing of the already heavily industrialized town, the lofty church, the beautiful town-houses and the various castles in the vicinity. One can see the light walls of the hermitage, the dark apertures, the blue roofs and the chimnies highlighted with brick-red. The clear composition, simple forms and homogeneous, thickly applied paint demonstrate a certain affinity with paintings by Cézanne during this same period. The discreet palette, mainly green and blue, attains much brightness through an Impressionistic technique.

Camille Pissarro (1830–1903)
The Hermitage at Pontoise. 1874
Oil on canvas. 61 × 81 cm
Purchased 1923

PAUL GAUGUIN's landscape *Blue Roofs* illustrates a phase of radical change in the style of the fourty year old artist. Beginning in 1879, he took part in the final four exhibitions of the group. In 1883 he moved to Rouen with his teacher Pissarro who then changed his address again the following year. Nevertheless, the unmistakeable influence of this brief encounter was still evident in Gauguin's paintings in 1885. The affinity of the two painters is made clear not only by their choice of motifs, but also by the composition and brushwork. The hook-like application of colour lends the meadow a grid-like effect, parallel lanes of hatched strokes follow the path in the foreground, and the sky could serve as a classic example of Impressionism. The houses stand out in contrast to their surroundings. For Pissarro in 1874, they represent an as yet incomplete change of direction towards the pure seeing of Impressionism, whereas ten years later they signify Gauguin's move away from it. The bright blue roofs, the paint applied thickly, are partially contoured by dark lines and thus stand out from the countryside, contrary to the precepts of Impressionism. The figure in the lower left-hand corner, moving into the scene, indicates the central role which the human being will be given in the Symbolism of Gauguin.

Paul Gauguin (1848–1903)
Blue Roofs. 1884
Oil on canvas. 74 × 60 cm
Purchased 1931

EDOUARD MANET never took part in the joint exhibitions of the Impressionists even though this had caused great concern to the organizers from the very beginning. Convinced that only the official Salon would lead to success, he tried to dissuade his friends from participation in the Impressionist exhibitions. Like Degas, Manet showed little interest in landscape painting which was one of the Impressionists' principal themes. «La vie moderne» became a key word for his art, a metaphor for life in the big city of the French metropolis. Manet's painting of 1878, *At the Café*, is devoted to this topic. It shows several guests at the Cabaret de Reichshoffen, seated at marble tables drinking beer. The two persons in the centre are acquaintances of the artist: the actress Ellen Andrée and the

Edouard Manet (1832–1883)
At the Café. 1878
Oil on canvas. 78 × 84 cm
Purchased 1953

97

engraver Henri Guérard. Werner Hofmann's comment on Edouard Manet's people in general is also applicable to this work: they are «spectators who put themselves on display»[44]. The source of light is directed incidentally at the brightly illuminated lady who is flanked by two gentlemen in top hats, thus lifting her out of the anonymity of the crowd. She is aware of the situation and plays both the role of the observer and at the same time fixes her beholder with a steadfast gaze. The left edge of the picture boldly cuts the composition, giving it the instantaneity of a photograph and robbing the man in the top hat, not without irony, of his face and personality. The others look but do not see one another, perhaps concentrating on a performance or on someone opposite them. This treatment of the subject suggests a state of rigidity from which no change can be expected. One may recognize in this scene a state of psychic isolation and abandonment of human beings caught up in the hustle and bustle of life in a big city.

Even though some of the questions raised by this painting are answered by the strange story of its origin, it remains ambiguous and paradoxical like most of Manet's works. Its clear structure, resulting from the strongly emphasized diagonals, disguises the fact that the initial conception of *At the Café* had been a different one.[45] Its fate is directly related to that of *Beer Waitress* (National Gallery, London). X-ray photographs have shown that both pictures had been joined in a single, large composition. With a first cut just to the right of Henri Guérard, Manet removed the left third of the painting. The right section showed the young woman in profile, a man across the table from her smoking, a waitress standing and other guests in the background. Apparently still not satisfied with the result, Manet removed the woman in profile from the right section and put her back in her original position on the left. Only after a horizontal cut at the top which reduced the height did *At the Café* attain its final format.

Manet's unconventional detail views could be the result of a mechanical reduction of the finished picture. This also explains *The Departure of the Steamship for Folkestone* where a few centimeters of the painted canvas extend beyond the canvas stretcher. The painting originated during a sojourn in Boulogne and shows the cross section of the scarcely identifiable steamship from an elevated viewpoint. Depth has been compressed into the surface plane, and people and objects are cut by the frame on all sides. The blurred crowd is indicated succintly by flocculent, flowing and rapid brushstrokes. In every respect, it is an experimental painting which enthralled Edgar Degas who acquired it in 1883 after Manet's death.

The *Portrait of Marguerite de Conflans with Headdress* is less flowing but extraordinarily masterful. A sparse, dry application of paint, underscored by hatching which Manet executed with the tip of the brush, reproduces the veil-like headdress. Manet's models were often friends or members of the family. Marguerite de Conflans sat for portraits by the artist on five occasions; she was befriended with Manet and his wife and attended the private concerts held by Madame Manet.

Manet concentrated on flower still lifes during two periods, from 1864 to 1865 and again towards the end of his life. While Manet considered still lifes in general during the first phase, he later confined his interest

[44] WERNER HOFMANN, *Nana. Mythos und Wirklichkeit*, Cologne 1973, p. 101.
[45] JULIET WILSON BAREAU, *The Hidden Face of Manet. An investigation of the artist's working processes*, exhib. cat. Courtauld Institute Galleries, London 1986, pp. 65–76.

Edouard Manet (1832–1883)
*Portrait of Marguerite de Conflans
with Headdress.* 1873
Oil on canvas. 55.5 × 46.5 cm
Purchased 1947

Edouard Manet (1832–1883)
*The Departure of the Steamship
for Folkestone.* 1869
Oil on canvas. 62 × 100.5 cm
Purchased 1923

Edouard Manet (1832–1883)
Flower Bouquet. 1882
Oil on canvas. 54 × 34.5 cm
Purchased 1923

Edgar Degas (1834–1917)
Dancer in Her Dressing Room. c. 1878/79
Pastel and gouache on cardboard
60 × 40 cm
Purchased 1923

to a few subjects only, at a time when he was already seriously ill. Sixteen simple flower arrangements of small size are central. *Flower Bouquet* belongs to this group and must have been completed in the spring of 1882. The choice of motif was influenced by Manet's faithful admirer Méry Laurent. During this period she had her maid deliver a daily bunch of flowers to the artist. The spring bouquet consisted of peonies, marigolds and lilacs and, as in almost all of the paintings of this series, was placed in a crystal vase on a light table top before a very dark background; its glistening light and luminous colour contrasts are captivating.

EDGAR DEGAS was that member of the group who was least pleased with the designation «impressionistes» and therefore insisted on «indépendants». Like Manet, he clearly dissociated himself from the themes of the landscapists. First and foremost, he was interested in the human figure and most especially in the dancer. She was to become the embodiment of his art. Approximately 1500 pastels, oil paintings, drawings and sculptures portray the dancer on the stage, at rehearsals and during intermissions or, as in the painting at «Römerholz», in the dressing room shortly before her appearance on stage. Characteristic of his works of the late 1870s, *Dancer in Her Dressing Room* represents a skillful technique which combines pastel and gouache.

It is true that for once the dancer herself is not cut, but Degas had almost never before chosen such a narrow section of a scene. The door on the right, in brown gouache, and the wall on the left boldly take up more than a third of the total pictorial field. A peep at the intimate scene through the door which stands ajar reveals the final preparations in the well-lit dressing room. Adorned with flowers, the dancer arranges her billowy pink tutu. An older, darkly clad woman hooks it up for her. A seated, uncouth admirer with a long nose, moustache and goatee observes the scene with the eye of an expert. Men of his type are usually portrayed in the same role by Degas: dark, often mere silhouettes, they observe the events with coarseness and passivity. Perspective, composition, light and the magic of colour are concentrated on the dancer whose tense ballet pose personifies vitality and grace.

As opposed to Renoir but in agreement with Manet, Degas' pictures also bear witness to the anonymity of city life: Turning away or shown in lost profile, in shadow or shining in their finery, it is only seldom that the individual's face is distinguishable. Contrasts of skin colour, costume textures, structures of the furnishings, and the distance achieved by «peeping through the keyhole» reduce the human figure to an interchangeable object of study for the artist. With startling frankness, he acknowledged: «No art is less spontaneous than mine. What I do is the result of reflecting upon and studying the great masters. Inspiration, spontaneity and temperament are unknown to me.»[46]

[46] EDGAR DEGAS, conversation with George Moore [before 1890], quoted from: Denys Sutton, Degas. Leben und Werk, Fribourg 1986, p. 309.

Cézanne, a Pioneer of Modern Painting

PAUL CÉZANNE too participated in the Impressionists' exhibitions. Stimulated by Pissarro, he devoted himself to the coloured appearance of the landscape. Strictly speaking, he was concerned with mere externals, the motifs and, to a certain degree, the technique of applying paint. For the most part, however, he always went his own way. Cézanne responded to Manet's virtuosity, which was comparable to that of the old masters, with an explosivness which can be likened only to the Expressionism of the twentieth century. Later he developed even further the style which reduced the optical appearance of forms to a sketch-like impression, to almost autonomous abstractions which transfer the motif into «harmony parallel with nature»[47]. Alongside van Gogh's expressiveness and the primitivism of Gauguin, Cézanne's abstraction is the most important forerunner of avant-garde at the beginning of the twentieth century.

Paul Cézanne (1839—1906)
Mont Sainte-Victoire. c. 1904—1906
Watercolour on paper. 47.2 × 62.6 cm
Purchased 1923

[47] PAUL CÉZANNE, conversation with Joachim Gasquet, quoted from: Paul Cézanne über die Kunst, ed. by Walter Hess, Mittenwald 1980, p. 12.

Cézanne created the outstanding early *Portrait of Dominique Aubert* about 1866. The seated man, holding his head, was Cézanne's uncle, an usher at court who at that time often sat for his nephew. In November 1866, the author Antony Valabrègue wrote to Emile Zola, a friend of Cézanne's since his youth, about the origins of this picture: «Fortunately, I only had to pose for one day. His uncle usually sits model for him. He finishes a portrait of him each afternoon.»[48] This impetuous tempo has nothing to do with virtuosic ease, rather the formative process is much more comparable to a volcanic eruption. Paint is applied or flung with the spatula – «style couillarde» was the name the artist supposedly gave to the technique. This method minimizes the facial features, as in caricature, reducing them to successions of wild strokes of the brush and patches of colour. This and the frankly dirty brown/black painting, which is clearly not palliative, reveals the vehement temperament of the young artist who mocks all conventionality. The portrait is an existential image. It was not the incidental, the individuality of the model, which interested Cézanne;

Paul Cézanne (1839–1906)
Portrait of Dominique Aubert. c. 1866
Oil on canvas. 81.5 × 66 cm
Purchased 1938

Paul Cézanne (1839–1906)
Self-Portrait. c. 1880
Oil on canvas. 33.5 × 24.5 cm
Purchased before 1936

rather it was the elementary existence of the subject and his own feelings and obsessions which Cézanne wanted to capture and which reveal themselves in like manner in the painting.

Among the painters, Cézanne was the one who was often consumed with self-doubt, just as Dürer, Rembrandt, van Gogh and Hodler had been. In the *Self-Portrait* of about 1880, the head, immovable like a block of stone, is placed into the small, quadratic format. The effect of the silent, withdrawn face is monumental. Despite their proximity, the very dark eyes and the mouth, almost completely hidden by a beard, convey distance. It is as if Cézanne were looking within and listening. He clearly distanced himself from the superficial charms and from the light-heartedness and flickering spontaneity of Monet and Renoir. Evidence of this is provided by the strongly expressive self portrait, clearly composed from a series of ordered strokes.

48 ANTONY VALABRÈGUE, letter to Emile Zola, November 1866, quoted from: Cézanne. Les années de jeunesse 1859–1872, exhib. cat. Musée d'Orsay, Paris 1988, p. 92.

During the course of Cézanne's artistic development, his motifs became increasingly abstract. This process can be followed in the series of exemplary still lifes at «Römerholz». Like Chardin, his important forerunner, still life provided Cézanne with scope for experimentation where he gave new expression to the relationships between shape and colour and the problem of light and space, independent of the traditional patterns of representation. The goal he realized by constant variation and transformation was described pointedly by Kandinsky in 1912: «It is not a person or an apple or a tree which is depicted. Rather Cézanne makes use of these objects in order to create a resonant image which, when realized, is called a picture.»[49] The *Still Life with Fruit Bowl and Apples* was painted at the same time as the *Self-Portrait*. The artist used a very specific type of brushstroke in both paintings which resulted in a stabilization of the picture's structure. As in Impressionism, there are no lines of division. However, Cézanne confronts that dynamic disintegration of forms with a clearly ordered succession of strokes which transforms one object into the next by a highly differentiated modulation of colour. All pictorial elements are embedded in a firmly ordered system which emantes tranquility.

Paul Cézanne (1839–1906)
Still Life with Fruit Bowl and Apples
c. 1879–1882
Oil on canvas. 55 × 74.5 cm
Purchased 1921

Rainer Maria Rilke's careful analysis of Cézanne's method of painting is exemplified by the unfinished *Still Life with Jug and Fruit* of about 1890: «Beginning with the darkest hues, he covered their intensity with a layer of colour which he extended somewhat beyond the underlying colour. Continuing in this manner, colour for colour, he arrived at another contrasting pictorial element, from which, as a new centre, he proceeded in like manner.»[50] The fruit make it especially clear how Cézanne, from various centres of the «darkest hues», produced bridges of colour. The care with which this process was carried out is striking. The tempestuousness of his early period is no longer evident. His paintings are now the product of extremely slow processes. Each new patch of colour is applied only when the artist is certain that it is a continuation of the previous, underlying colour tone. Thus, the work exhibits harmony at each stage on its way to completion.

Paul Cézanne (1839–1906)
Still Life with Jug and Fruit. c. 1890
Oil on canvas. 46 × 55 cm
Bequest of Werner Reinhart 1951

[49] WASSILY KANDINSKY, *Über das Geistige in der Kunst* [1912], Bern-Bümpliz ⁴1952, S. 51.
[50] RAINER MARIA RILKE, letter to Clara Rilke, 9 October 1907, in: R. M. R., *Briefe aus den Jahren 1906 bis 1907*, Leipzig 1930, p. 365.

Paul Cézanne (1839–1906)
Still Life with Peaches. c. 1892
Oil on canvas. 32.5 × 41 cm
Purchased 1923

The simplicity and clarity with which the fruit are arranged on the plate in *Still Life with Peaches* of about 1892 is reminiscent of Chardin. The large *Still Life with Faience Jug* (c. 1900) portrays the plate of fruits as an element of a four part baroque-like composition. The red apples on a light coloured plate are embedded on a dark curtain which falls in gathers onto the table. Next to it stands a rounded faience jug, a crystal goblet and still more apples lying on and around a second white cloth. The manner in which Cézanne uses patches of colour as building blocks determines not only the representation, but also creates a new reality, that «mental resonance of an image which is called a picture» (Kandinsky).

With this, Cézanne paved the way for abstraction and, at the same time, severed the bonds with traditional perspective. The pictorial space is not conceived from just one focal point, rather the objects are represented from different viewpoints and perspectives: The plate from the left, the jug from the front, the apples on the cloth from the right. This leads to a compression of depth and to an emphasis of the picture plane, thus anticipating the simultaneity of Cubism.

In his famous letter to Emile Bernard, Cézanne talks about abstraction and new conceptions of space and advised Bernard to: «see in nature the cylinder, the sphere and the cone, putting everything in proper per-

Paul Cézanne (1839–1906)
Still Life with Faience Jug. c. 1900
Oil on canvas. 73 × 100.5 cm
Purchased 1925

[51] PAUL CÉZANNE, letter to Emile Bernard, 15 April 1904, quoted from: Paul Cézanne. Briefe, ed. by John Rewald, Zurich 1979, p. 281.

Paul Cézanne (1839–1906)
Château Noir. c. 1890
Oil on canvas. 73.5 × 92.5 cm
Purchased 1926

Paul Cézanne (1839–1906)
Pilon du Roi. 1887 / 1888
Oil on canvas. 81.5 × 100.5 cm
Purchased 1923

spective so that each side of an object or a plane is directed toward a central point.»[51] In the two magnificent landscapes, *Château Noir* and *Pilon du Roi*, nature being the model is transformed in the painting into a «harmony which parallels nature». In practice, of course, Cézanne did not insist on composing this harmony from cylinders, spheres and cones. Rather his building blocks, out of which he created a new order, were the areas of colour, evenly applied with parallel brushstrokes. In this manner he coverd the surface of the canvas, uniting proximity and distance to give a new reality. It is only our way of seeing which enables us to perceive objects in these relationships between forms. Thus the programmatic words of Maurice Denis in 1890 are relevant to the late works of Cézanne: «One must realize that before a painting is a charger, a nude or an anecdote, it is a surface covered with colours that are combined into a certain arrangement.»[52]

In the surroundings of his home in Aix-en-Provence, Cézanne returned time and again to the same places: the Château Noir, the Pilon du Roi and *Mont Sainte-Victoire* (p. 103). A late watercolour of the latter is found at «Römerholz». The continuous contact with these motifs is what enabled him to express their timeless validity, to «bring Poussin to life through nature»[53]. The *Bathers* is a recurring theme in which Cézanne sings praises to his ideal of a paradisiacal accord between man and nature. This watercolour of 1895–1900 is one of his most beautiful; the female nudes are painted in brilliant colours with an unusually dynamic, easy brushstroke so that they become interwoven with the landscape.

Paul Cézanne (1839–1906)
Women Bathing. 1895–1900
Watercolour on paper. 22.7 × 35.8 cm
Purchased 1923

[52] MAURICE DENIS, *Définition du néo-traditionnisme* [1890], in: M. D., Du symbolisme au classicisme. Théories, Paris 1964, p. 33.
[53] PAUL CÉZANNE, conversation with Joachim Gasquet, quoted from: Paul Cézanne über die Kunst, ed. by Walter Hess, Mittenwald 1980, p. 63.

Postimpressionism

HENRI DE TOULOUSE-LAUTREC was, almost exclusively, a portraitist. He took up the motifs of Honoré Daumier, Edouard Manet and Edgar Degas and broadened their glimpse behind the scenes of bourgeois respectability to include a still more ruthless observation of the individual. Toulouse-Lautrec's origin and background have contributed to the legend which has grown up around him: The pathetic picture of a crippled, dwarf-like descendant of a once powerful line of counts who now identified with society's outcasts. This image, together with the cliché that Toulouse-Lautrec never really forgot his status were intended to explain a note of aristocracy in his art. Lautrec has made a lasting and determining mark with his brilliant drawings which expose tabooed reality, without contempt, revealing the emotional state of his models to a greater extent than his precursors had done.

The *Lady Clown Cha-U-Kao* (p. 114) was a dancer at the Moulin Rouge and acrobat at the Nouveau Cirque in Paris. Beginning in 1895, Lautrec painted several portraits of her. A colour lithograph of 1897 is a direct transposition of this painting which, however, does not equal its profound psychological expression. «Chahut-chaos», the name of the dance she performed at the Moulin Rouge, complies in its written, phonetic form with her oriental sounding stage-name, Cha-U-Kao. Contemporary photographs show a young, attractive woman posing as a supple acrobat or frivolously displaying her bare bosom. As the «Römerholz» picture discloses, Toulouse-Lautrec saw this woman in a completely different light. He portrays the clown in a free and easy pose, swaggering like a man; she is lost in thought and takes no notice of the spectator. Contempt of men and disillusion are written all over her face. Her low-cut, ruffled costume and the pert little cap do not hide the signs of grief. Her companion, with whom she crosses the foyer of the Moulin Rouge, may remind her of her own future. One cannot imagine that this respectable old woman, who has lost her figure, had once known fame as «Gabrielle la Danseuse». The public in the background takes no notice of the two women, its attention is captured by the entertainment. Singled out by the yellow pillar, the man in profile, wearing a bowler, has been identified as Lautrec's friend, Tristan Bernard. Whereas the crowd of spectators forms an entity with its surroundings, the women seem to lose their balance and tip away from the vertical axis. Thus, the composition calls attention to their role as outsiders.

Henri de Toulouse-Lautrec (1864–1901)
The Lady Clown Cha-U-Kao. 1895
Oil on canvas. 75 × 55 cm
Purchased 1922

Three oil paintings from Arles highlight the works of VINCENT VAN GOGH at «Römerholz». The important counterparts, *The Courtyard of the Hospital in Arles* and *The Sick-Ward of the Hospital in Arles*, were painted after van Gogh's internment in this hospital and his gradual convalescence in April 1889. The *Portrait of Augustine Roulin* was painted at the end of November or the beginning of December 1888, just before Gauguin's departure, the event which had contributed substantially to van Gogh's collapse. In the summer of that year, the artist created two ink drawings, *Garden in the Provence* and *View of Les Saintes-Maries-de-la-Mer* (p. 116). Both show an energetic brushstroke and compositional completion, so that they cannot be considered to be studies. The earliest painting by van Gogh in the collection, *Still Life with Herrings, Tomatoes and Lemons*, goes back to the beginning of his stay in Paris. It is one of the first works which Oskar Reinhart acquired after the death of his father in 1919.

Vincent van Gogh (1853–1890)
Still Life with Herrings, Tomatoes and Lemons. 1886
Oil on canvas. 38 × 55 cm
Purchased 1919

The range of colours in this fish still life does not suggest that it was painted in Paris. It shows no signs whatsoever of a confrontation with Impressionism, and its dark tonality recalls the paintings executed in Holland. In fact, this work must have originated in the month of his arrival in Paris, before he entered the Cormon Studio in April 1886. At this time, the artist was aware of the Impressionists only through hearsay. His greatest prototypes were the Provençal painter, Adolphe Monticelli and Delacroix who, he asserted, adhered to the same theory of colour. Typical of these artists were complementary contrasts on a dark background, a feature found in this still life. Just after the picture's completion, the eighth and final Impressionist exhibition opened its doors, and van Gogh gradually entered into a new phase of experimentation. Impressionism, Pointillism and Japonism brought a lighter range of colour tones and new discoveries of painting techniques; this quickly lead to a personal synthesis.

Vincent van Gogh (1853–1890)
Portrait of Augustine Roulin. 1888
Oil on canvas. 54 × 65 cm
Purchased 1925

The *Portrait of Augustine Roulin* was painted along with other likenesses of the Roulin family in November or at the beginning of December 1888, as reported by van Gogh to his brother Theo. The postal clerk Roulin and his wife were the only persons in Arles who were concerned about the odd painter. At the same time, Gauguin, who had just arrived from Pont-Aven, also painted Madame Roulin in a green dress, seated before a yellow background. His influence on van Gogh's work reveals itself in the daring limitation to three basic colour tones and with respect to the painting technique: The green dress is painted quite flatly, contoured in complementary tones of red and brown – a characteristic of Gauguin's «cloisonnisme». The bold variation in tones of yellow, from mustard to sulfur to lemon yellow may be understood as a transposition of the experiences made in depicting the sunflowers from which Gauguin, on the other hand, profited considerably. Van Gogh's preoccupation with the Japanese woodcut is revealed by the section of window. Rejecting customary rules of perspective – pots of bulbs become gigantic, a path winds into the sky – led to flat, purely decorative effects. Madame Roulin is seated in the chair which Vincent had placed in Gauguin's room prior to his arrival and which, concurrent with this work, he portrayed empty as if he were anticipating his friend's impending departure.

From the hospital at Arles, van Gogh wrote to his sister Willemien at the end of April that he had painted two pictures: «L'un une salle, une très longue salle avec les rangées de lits à rideaux blancs où se mouvent quelques figures de malades [...]. Et alors comme pendant la cour inté-

Vincent van Gogh (1853–1890)
View of Les Saintes-Maries-de-la-Mer. 1888
Quill pen and Indian ink on paper
43.5 × 60 cm
Purchased after 1926

Vincent van Gogh (1853–1890)
Garden in the Provence. 1888
Quill pen and Indian ink on paper
49 × 61 cm
Purchased after 1926

Vincent van Gogh (1853–1890)
The Sick-Ward of the Hospital in Arles. 1889
Oil on canvas. 72 × 91 cm
Purchased 1925

rieure.»[54] («One of a room, a very long room with rows of white cur-tained beds along the walls; some of the sick are walking about [...]. And then as a pendant, the courtyard.») Accordingly, *The Sick-Ward of the Hospital in Arles* must have been painted first – but in the form described here: The composition originally showed the long aisle, the beds, and a few patients strolling about. Not until October 1889, in the clinic of St. Rémy, did it receive its present appearance. A literary experience was the determining factor, as the artist himself emphasized: «J'avais lu un ar-ticle sur Dostojevsky qui avait écrit un livre Souvenirs de la maison des morts et cela m'avait poussé à reprendre une grande étude que j'avais [faite: corrected to] commencée dans la salle des fiévreux à Arles.»[55] («I read an article about Dostojewski who had written a book 'Memories of the morgue'; this motivated me to work again on a large study that I [made: corrected to] begun in the delirium-ward at Arles.») The boldly cut off stove, projected two-dimensionally, and the group of patients gathered around it were added later, as proven by Roland Dorn. The floor too was touched up; its chopped, fan-like hatching intensifies the oppres-sive effect of the flat perspective of the aisle. It seems to go uphill in this room; one asks oneself if one will ever reach the door at the other end,

above which hangs a crucifix. People are seated around the stove, with-drawn and waiting, not knowing for what.

In its counterpart, *The Courtyard of the Hospital in Arles*, van Gogh painted spring in a colourful luminosity, «like someone who no longer believed that he would ever see it again»[56]. The Impressionistic treatment of the flower beds intensifies in the lower third of the picture into an agi-tated brushstroke. In contrast, the gallery on which the patients are to be seen, painted quietly and opaquely, appears to be a permanent, inescap-able structure. What is more, cutting off the view on all sides, allowing neither a prospect of open landscape nor the trees to grow towards the open sky, arouses an oppressive feeling of imprisonment. In his descrip-tion of this scene in the above-mentioned letter to his sister, one comment stands out particularly: «C'est donc un tableau tout plein de fleurs et de verdure printanière. Trois troncs d'arbres noirs et tristes cependant le tra-versent comme des serpents et sur le premier plan quatre grands buissons tristes de buis sombres.»[57] («Thus, it is a picture replete with flowers and the greenery of springtime. And yet, three black, dismal tree trunks cut across it like snakes, and in the foreground four large, woeful shrubs of boxwood.») Sadness lurks even in this blossoming garden.

Vincent van Gogh (1853–1890)
The Courtyard of the Hospital in Arles. 1889
Oil on canvas. 73 × 92 cm
Purchased 1923

[54] VINCENT VAN GOGH, letter to Wille-mien, end of April 1889, quoted from: Roland Dorn, Décoration. Vincent van Goghs Werkreihe für das Gelbe Haus in Arles, Hildesheim/Zurich/New York 1990, p. 473.
[55] VINCENT VAN GOGH, letter to Wille-mien, 15 October 1889, quoted from: R. Dorn, op. cit. p. 474. Based on this hand-written insert, Dorn was able to point out the later overpainting.
[56] LISBETH STÄHELIN, *Sammlung Oskar Reinhart Winterthur*, Braunschweig 1983 [museum], p. 79.
[57] VINCENT VAN GOGH, letter to Wille-mien, end of April 1889, quoted from: R. Dorn, op. cit., p. 472.

Edouard Vuillard (1868–1940)
Two Women at the Table. c. 1900–1904
Oil on canvas. 46 × 56.5 cm
Purchased 1949

Works by Vuillard, Utrillo and Picasso chronologically round off the Oskar Reinhart Collection. Vuillard and Utrillo stand completely under the influence of late Impressionism, while an early portrait and three Ingres-like drawings by Picasso document a vital involvement with earlier epochs and revive a recurring theme of the collection: the contrasts between painting and drawing.

EDOUARD VUILLARD depicts *Two Women at the Table.* In this work of about 1900–1904, the influence of Pierre Bonnard is evident. Compared with Vuillard's unmistakable originality and planar stylization of the Nabis period, and despite its free, sketchy disintegration of form, this picture is a rebirth of Impressionism. Glasses and carafe, bowls of fruit, knives and plates dissolve in the play of light on the dazzling white table-

cloth. Dark accents are set by the figures who are seated obliquely opposite. They too are depicted in an extremely sketchy manner. It remains speculation as to whether they portray Vuillard's mother and sister.

Impressionism also experiences a revival in the effervescent light of *Moulin de la Galette in Snow* by MAURICE UTRILLO. This snowscape of about 1917 is virtually a pendant to Vuillard's interior in white. Utrillo painted the famous windmill of Montmartre time and again. As if covered by a veil, the scene is transfigured by the blanket of snow; the painting is considered to be one of Utrillo's best. The snow relieves the tension between the city on the one hand, eating its way into the countryside, and the rural idyll at the edge of the metropolis, as expressed by van Gogh in his paintings of the Moulin de la Galette.

Maurice Utrillo (1883–1955)
Moulin de la Galette in Snow. c. 1917
Oil on canvas. 33 × 46 cm
Purchased 1946

Pablo Picasso (1881–1973)
Portrait of Mateu Fernández de Soto. 1901
Oil on canvas. 61 × 46.5 cm
Purchased 1935

The final climax of the collection is provided by the works of PABLO PICASSO. The *Portrait of Mateu Fernández de Soto* is not only one of the most important of Picasso's early portraits, it is also a key to the biography of his first stay in Paris. The subject of this portrait is the young Spanish sculptor, Mateu de Soto, whom Picasso had met in Barcelona in 1899. The portrait was painted at the onset of the winter of 1901 when de Soto, destitute and hungry, to whom every success was to be denied, was taken in by Picasso. It shows the sculptor seated at a table, completely withdrawn. His eyes seem to be closed even though he is fashioning a small sculpture with a modelling tool. As can often be observed in male likenesses of this phase, Picasso has represented de Soto as one of El Greco's saints: unworldly, entranced and, typical of this prototype, with exaggerated elongations. The expressively painted portrait reveals too the extreme rapidity with which Picasso appropriated the art of Impressionism and Postimpressionism in Paris. Thematically, the portrait follows the iconography of the lonesome alcoholic and the desperate ones in the

works of Manet, Degas, van Gogh and Toulouse-Lautrec. However, Picasso has not simply varied this theme; he has basically expanded on it by adding a personal dimension. He is standing on the threshold of the Blue Period, stylistically and especially with regard to colour.

The partial image which Picasso inserted in the background originated six months earlier. It refers to *The Dead One* (Private Collection), a work that alludes to an event of great significance in the life of the young Picasso – the suicide of his painter friend, Carlos Casagemas who shot himself in the company of his friends in February 1901 during Picasso's absence. Picasso was existentially affected by the death of Casagemas; he felt himself partially responsible for it and attempted to come to terms with this event in numerous paintings. The monochrome blue painting and its subject-matter of melancholy and grief was basically triggered by this experience of death; it was in this period that Picasso found his way to absolute autonomy.

Picasso is without a doubt the most innovative artist of the twentieth century. A particular style held his interest only as long as he could acquire new forms of expression from it. After he had paved the way with Cubism for the avant-garde of the twentieth century, a classical phase of monumental figures began, as demonstrated by the drawing *Nursing Mother* in the matter-of-factness of her archaic corporeality. This change of direction was unleashed by a trip to Italy and recourse to Ingres' «beauty of line». The drawing testifies to the fact that Picasso was also one of the greatest draughtsman of our century.

Pablo Picasso (1881–1973)
Nursing Mother. 1919
Pencil on paper. 30.5 × 46.5 cm
Purchased 1919

Sculpture around 1900

In addition to paintings and drawings, the Oskar Reinhart Collection encompasses a small group of sculptures. Its main focus is on the works of Auguste Rodin, Pierre-Auguste Renoir, Aristide Maillol and Charles Despiau, to which the figures in the park by Antoine Bourdelle, Renée Sintenis and Hermann Hubacher can be added.

AUGUSTE RODIN is the most significant sculptor from the turn of the century. His topic is the human figure. He sought, like Delacroix, to illustrate extreme conditions of human existence, rapture and despair, by dramatic movements of the body. Within the context of his commitment to Romanticism, he grew sensitive to the fleeting, superficial stimuli of the Impressionists who were his contemporaries; on the other hand, formal innovations such as the fragmentation and deformation of the figure and abandonment of the pedestal point the way to the future.

Rodin created the *Study of a Seated Woman* in 1889. The equilibrium of the fragmented female body, leaning backwards, is highly complex. The delicate balance of the body is maintained by the slightly raised left leg and by the right arm, bent so that the hand touches the shoulder. The surface of the torso is not smooth. Curvatures and depressions, bulges and grooves bring about a flickering unrest since light does not strike the body evenly; rather, there is a constant play of light and shadow. However, Rodin was not concerned solely with surface effects. The physical movement of the figure communicates the force of inner energy and its externalization and is, therefore, an expression of emotion. *Study of a Seated Woman* is the model for a torso three times its size, *Kybele*, mother of the gods, on which Rodin worked until 1905 (casts in the Tate Gallery, London, and Musée des Beaux-Arts, Bordeaux). Each part of this body expresses utmost excitation, as described pertinently by Rodin's secretary, Rainer Maria Rilke: «The smallest part of the body revealed what was written on the face [...]; every spot was a mouth which said it in its own way», and: «Rodin seized life that he saw wherever he looked. He seized it in its most minute details, he observed it, he followed it. He waited for it at crossings where it hesitated, he caught up with it wherever it ran, and found it everywhere, always great, powerful, and enthralling. For no part of the body was insignificant or petty: it lived.»[58]

Auguste Rodin (1840–1917)
Study of a Seated Woman. 1889
Bronze. Height 50.5 cm
Date of purchase unknown

Aristide Maillol (1861–1944)
The Mediterranean. 1905
Limestone. 116 × 105 × 72 cm
Purchased 1931

[58] RAINER MARIA RILKE, *Auguste Rodin* [1902], Leipzig 1920, pp. 28 and 17–18.

Aristide Maillol (1861–1944)
Female Torso. 1906
Lead. Height 105 cm
Date of purchase unknown
Purchased 1931

Like Rodin, ARISTIDE MAILLOL was preoccupied for a lifetime with the nude, human figure. However, he pursued totally different goals in his realization of form and content. For this reason, he has been designated the counterpole to Rodin. Maillol's static, tranquil Neoclassicism was the antithesis of Rodin's dynamics. «Sculpture for me is a block»[59] – with block-like forms, smooth surfaces and elementary, simple positions of the body, Maillol sought to express timelessness. His major works are to be found in Winterthur, *The Mediterranean* and *Female Torso* at «Römerholz» and *Night* in the Kunstmuseum.

Maillol's first monumental sculpture, *The Mediterranean* (1905; p. 124), was admired by Rodin as an absolutely pure and modern masterpiece. Maillol had struggled at length with the motiv of the seated figure, probably going as far back as Gauguin's painting *Aha Oe Feii?* (1892; Puschkin Museum of Fine Arts, Moscow). In drawings, a tapestry and numerous small pieces of sculpture, one of which is at «Römerholz», he studied the proportions and distribution of masses with the aim of attaining perfect harmony. The profile of the seated figure takes the form of a triangle, and even the sensitive play between the volume of the powerful body and voids which surround the body parts is based on triangular forms. Its tectonic structure is of lapidary clarity. The relationships between forms unite in a closed corporeal architecture whose static repose expresses elementary being. André Gide described this effect in 1905: «How beautifully the light rests on this shoulder! How beautifully the shadow lies on the slope of this brow! No thought causes it to furrow; no passion causes these mighty breasts to tremble.»[60]

The stone figure, *The Mediterranean*, and the lead cast, *Female Torso*, which followed a year later, embody the scope of Maillol's art. He was commissioned in 1905 to produce a monument in honour of the social revolutionary, Auguste Blanqui (1805–1881). The memorial, *The Enchained Act*, in Puget-Théniers near Grenoble portrays a colossal female figure, larger than life, who, twisting and turning, uses all her strength to burst the chains with which her hands are bound to her back. This symbol of the imprisoned revolutionary is very expressive. It is merely the reduction of this figure to a torso which transforms the allegorical event into a sculptural one: Suspense and power are not transmitted in the narrative sense but manifest themselves in the body itself.

The sculptor Maillol carefully studied the plastic power of PIERRE-AUGUSTE RENOIR's neoclassically painted nudes: «Look at Renoir's nudes: they are pure sculpture.»[61] On the other hand, Renoir admired Maillol's animated confrontation with antiquity. Ambroise Vollard, one of Renoir's art dealers, encouraged Renoir to try his hand at sculpturing. He placed Maillol's young pupil, Richard Guino, at his disposal from 1913–1917. Renoir, who was suffering from progressive arthritis, was no longer in a position to do the modelling himself. He directed Guino from a wheelchair in transforming the themes of his paintings into free-standing sculptures and reliefs.

Mother and Child is the plastic conversion of the theme *Nursing Mother* from the year 1885: At that time, Renoir had transfigured his wife Aline, who was nursing their firstborn son Pierre, into the epitome of primeval motherhood in a series of drawings and paintings. After her death in 1915, Renoir took up the subject again. The statuette produced in 1916

[59] ARISTIDE MAILLOL, quoted from: Eduard Trier, Bildhauertheorien im 20. Jahrhundert, Berlin 1984, p. 53.
[60] ANDRÉ GIDE, *Promenade au Salon d'Automne*, in: Gazette des Beaux-Arts 34, 1905, pp. 478–479.
[61] ARISTIDE MAILLOL, quoted from: Paul Haesaerts, Renoir Sculpteur, New York 1947, p. 15.

Pierre-Auguste Renoir (1841–1919)
Large Laundress, Kneeling. 1917
Bronze. 123 × 55 × 135 cm
Date of purchase unknown

Pierre-Auguste Renoir (1841–1919)
Mother and Child. 1916
Bronze. Height 55 cm
Date of purchase unknown

was a study for a never realized full-scale sculpture intended for Aline's grave. Under Renoir's attentive guidance, Guino used a modelling tool to create a surface structure which closely resembles the loose and easy brushwork of the painting.

Large Laundress, Kneeling is one of Renoir's principal sculptures. Guino modelled it in 1917 according to a small study, a bronze cast of which is found at «Römerholz». Bathers and laundresses are favourite themes of Renoir's late works. In constrast to the painted versions of 1912 that portray clothed women in an idyllic river landscape, Renoir chose an Arcadian, nude figure for the statue. Neither in the paintings nor in the sculptures was Renoir interested in the physical labour of laundresses. Hence, the cloth which the kneeling figure is holding is merely a thematic pretext for this position as well as a formal means of capturing the raised arm gesture and of merging it with the figure into an integral whole.

Bibliography

Index

KARL SCHEFFLER, *Die Sammlung Oskar Reinhart in Winterthur*, in: Kunst und Künstler 25, 1926, pp. 2–13

PIERRE COURTHION, *La collection Oskar Reinhart [Les collections privées en Suisse I]*, in: L'Amour de l'Art 7, 1926, pp. 1–24

WALDEMAR GEORGE, *Collection Oskar Reinhart. Topographie d'une collection*, in: Formes 1932, nos. 26/27

JULIUS MEIER-GRAEFE, *Die Sammlung Oskar Reinhart*, in: Frankfurter Zeitung, April 29, 1932 and May 12, 1932

RICHARD SEIFFERT-WATTENBERG, *Aus der Sammlung Oskar Reinhart*, Munich 1935

Reden gehalten bei Anlass der Eröffnung der Ausstellung «Sammlung Oskar Reinhart» im Kunstmuseum Bern, den 16. Dezember 1939 by the president of the Swiss Confederation PHILIPP ETTER, by F. V. FISCHER, lawyer, by Dr. h. c. OSKAR REINHART and by ERNST BÄRTSCHI, mayor, Berne 1939

Sammlung Oskar Reinhart Winterthur, foreword by CONRAD VON MANDACH, catalogue by HEINZ KELLER, exhibition catalogue Kunstmuseum Bern, 1939–1940

Sammlung Oskar Reinhart. Alte Meister und französische Maler des 19. Jahrhunderts, introduction by WILHELM WARTMANN, exhibition catalogue Kunsthaus Zurich, December 1940–March 1941

Die Privatsammlung Oskar Reinhart, introduction by GOTTHARD JEDLICKA, catalogue by HEINZ KELLER, biographies by LISBETH STÄHELIN, exhibition catalogue Kunstmuseum Winterthur, August–November 1955

GOTTHARD JEDLICKA, *An den Rand geschrieben. Divagationen über Bilder der Sammlung Oskar Reinhart*, in: Du, 1956, no. 8, pp. 5–51

RICHARD HÄSLI, *Oskar Reinhart. Zum 80. Geburtstag (11. Juni)*, in: Neue Zürcher Zeitung, June 11, 1965, no. 2502

RICHARD HÄSLI, *Oskar Reinhart †*, in: Neue Zürcher Zeitung, September 17, 1965, no. 3843

LISBETH STÄHELIN, *Dr. h. c. Oskar Reinhart (1885–1965)*, in: Schweizer Monatshefte 46, 1966, pp. 941–946

Sammlung Oskar Reinhart Am Römerholz, published by the Swiss Confederation, catalogue entries by LISBETH STÄHELIN, Winterthur 1970, ²1975, French edition 1971, English edition 1978

Eröffnung der Sammlung Oskar Reinhart «Am Römerholz» in Winterthur. 7. März 1970, addresses by URS WIDMER, mayor, by MICHAEL STETTLER and by the president of the Swiss Confederation HANS PETER TSCHUDI, Winterthur 1971

LISBETH STÄHELIN, *Fünf Bildnisse der «Sammlung Oskar Reinhart Am Römerholz», Winterthur*, in: Gotthard Jedlicka. Eine Gedenkschrift. Beiträge zur Kunstgeschichte des 19. und 20. Jahrhunderts, edited by Eduard Hüttinger and Hans A. Lüthy, Zurich 1974, pp. 47–57

RUDOLF KOELLA, *Die Sammlung Oskar Reinhart*, contributions by MICHAEL STETTLER and EDUARD HÜTTINGER, Zurich 1975, French edition: Neuchâtel 1975

RUDOLF KOELLA, *Sammlung Oskar Reinhart Am Römerholz*, Basle 1975 [Schweizerische Kunstführer]

FRANZ ZELGER, *Museums Discovered. The Oscar Reinhart Collections*, New York 1981

LISBETH STÄHELIN, *Sammlung Oskar Reinhart Winterthur*, Brunswick 1983 [museum]